NELSON MANDELA

D0313073

"NO EASY WALK TO FREEDOM"

A BIOGRAPHY BY
BARRY DENENBERG

■SCHOLASTIC

To all those who took the time to write –
you are my inspiration.

Scholastic Children's Books
Euston House, 24 Eversholt Street
London NW1 1DB

A division of Scholastic Ltd
London ~ New York ~ Toronto ~ Sydney ~ Auckland
Mexico City ~ New Delhi ~ Hong Kong

Published in the UK by Scholastic Ltd, 2014

Cover design by Kay Petronio
Book design by Will Denton
Photo research by Alan Gottlieb

ISBN 978 1407 14758 1

Printed and bound by CPI Group (UK) Ltd, Croydon, CR0 4YY

2 4 6 8 10 9 7 5 3 1

NELSON MANDELA

"NO EASY WALK TO FREEDOM"

CONTENTS

PART 4: STATE OF EMERGENCY

PART 5: FREE MANDELA

PART 6: THE STRUGGLE CONTINUES

PART 7: AFTER MANDELA

"No Easy Walk to Freedom" is from a speech by Nelson Mandela given September 21, 1953. The quotation was adapted from an article by Jawaharlal Nehru:

There is no easy walk to freedom anywhere, and many of us will have to pass through the valley of the shadow of death again and again before we reach the mountaintops of our desires.

AFRICA

SOUTH AFRICA: AN INTRODUCTION

South Africa is about five times the size of Great Britain. It is situated at the southern tip of the African continent, surrounded on three sides by ocean. Lying south of the equator it has, in general, a warm, sunny climate. The landscape is as beautiful as it is varied, including some of the best beaches in the world. It is divided into four provinces: the Cape Province, the Transvaal, the Orange Free State and Natal.

It is blessed with natural wealth, making it the richest country in Africa. More gold is produced by South Africa than by any other country in the world. Diamonds are another important source of South Africa's economic strength. Almost every important mineral is found there.

Although it represents only four per cent of the continent's land and six per cent of its population, it is the most highly developed country in Africa.

The first heart transplant operation was performed in South Africa. Its medical facilities are the best in the world.

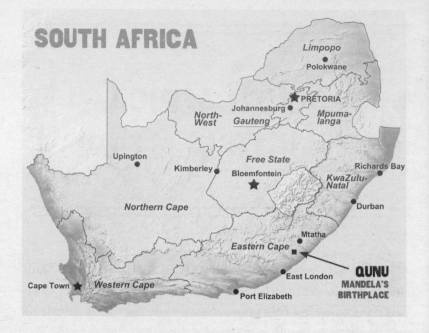

SOUTH AFRICA

Limpopo
Polokwane
PRETORIA
Johannesburg
North-West
Gauteng
Mpuma-langa
Upington
Free State
Richards Bay
Kimberley
Bloemfontein
KwaZulu-Natal
Northern Cape
Durban
Mtatha
Eastern Cape
QUNU
MANDELA'S
BIRTHPLACE
East London
Cape Town
Western Cape
Port Elizabeth

But South Africa is not known for any of these things. Primarily it has been known for its history of government policies toward the black African majority. Black South Africans had been enslaved, exploited, oppressed, tortured and killed by the white South African government for over a hundred years.

Until April 1994, South Africa's white citizens, numbering five million, ruled the country, even though they represented only fourteen per cent of the population.

South Africa has become known as the home of the world's most famous former political prisoner. A prisoner who emerged to become an internationally respected statesman. This is his story and the story of his country.

PART 1:
ROOTS

1
AFRICAN BOYHOOD

Rolihlahla is Nelson Mandela's tribal name. He was born on July 18, 1918. In Xhosa, the language that his parents spoke, Rolihlahla means 'one who brings trouble on himself'.

Nelson grew up in a valley surrounded by grass-covered hills. His village, Qunu, was located in the Transkei territory of South Africa. The youngest and only boy of four children, he and his father cared for the cattle and sheep, and Nelson helped when it was time to plough the fields. When his chores were done, he played football and learned to hunt and to fight with sticks.

As much as anything he enjoyed listening silently to his elders talk of African history. At meetings, after the chiefs and other important people from the surrounding areas had completed their business, they would sit and tell stories – stories of long ago, before the whites came to Africa. They also told stories of wars between the white man and the black man and how the white men stole the blacks' cattle and drove the blacks from their own land.

Transkei territory, where Mandela was born; Mandela's own home is no longer standing.

His father was the chief counsellor to the Paramount Chief of their tribe – the Thembu. The Paramount Chief himself was related to him, and his great-grandfather had been a king.

When he was twelve, his father died. Before he died, he saw to it that his son was placed in the care of an uncle, who was also a tribal chief. His parents had already seen how eager he was to learn, and his uncle was asked to provide him with a good education.

Understandably, when he first arrived at his new village, he kept to himself. But soon he grew more comfortable. His uncle's wife loved him as much as she loved her own child, whose name was Justice. He and Justice became like brothers. They hunted birds, using slings, and roamed and romped in the fields. Best of all, they enjoyed racing on horseback.

As before, he worked hard, herding the cattle, milking the cows, and he was always ready to lend a hand. He was well behaved and diligent in his studies.

The church schools he attended were run by missionaries. Christian missionaries had been coming to Africa for over fifteen hundred years. Their mission was to convert Africans to Christianity. Some missionaries tried to convince the Africans to accept foreign rule. But many worked to provide them with a Western education. Sometimes schools run by the missionaries were the only ones available, and in many cases included children of all races.

Like his mother, Rolihlahla became a good Christian. He studied English, the Xhosa language, history and geography. His teachers were very good, and he received the education his father had hoped he would.

When he was twenty, he enrolled at Fort Hare College, one of the few universities in South Africa that allowed full-time black students. It was located in the quiet town of Alice, in the Cape Province.

He was interested in politics and current affairs and thought he might become a lawyer. By studying law he might be able to help his people obtain the rights denied them by the white rulers.

He studied hard at Fort Hare, although he still had time to learn the fox-trot and the waltz. It wasn't long, however, before he became involved in politics. He joined the Students' Representative Council, which was organizing

Nelson Mandela at age nineteen in the Transkei.

a protest against the living conditions at the university. When the students decided to strike, he joined them and was expelled.

His uncle wanted him to apologize to the university authorities. He urged him to abandon the student boycott and continue his studies. By now it was clear to Rolihlahla that he was being groomed to someday take his rightful place as a tribal chief.

His uncle also thought it was time for him to marry. According to the custom of the time, his relative arranged the marriage. The bride had already been chosen. Rolihlahla had no choice. If he wanted to avoid the marriage he had to run away. Like many boys his age he headed for the bright lights and big city of Johannesburg.

In Johannesburg he would seek a different destiny. He would become a lawyer and work to free his people.

Although he preferred his clan name, Madiba, he used the European name his missionary schoolteacher gave him at the age of seven. The name by which he would become known to people all over the world.

Nelson.

Nelson Mandela.

2

EGOLI – CITY OF GOLD

In 1941, when Mandela was twenty-three, Johannesburg was well on its way to becoming one of the world's most modern cities. Africans called it Egoli – City of Gold. Sixty years earlier gold had been discovered, and the city had grown rapidly. Hundreds of thousands of Africans from the surrounding rural areas migrated to Johannesburg, hoping to find work in the factories and the mines.

Mandela took a job as a guard outside one of the compounds where the black miners were housed. Armed with a whistle and a knobbed stick, he was there to make sure everyone behaved themselves. The living conditions shocked him. Miners were not allowed to have their families with them. Food and shelter were provided, but not much else. If you quit you risked being sent to jail. There were no sick days, holidays or pensions. The men slept sometimes fifty to a room, on double-decker concrete bunks, and hid their belongings at night so they wouldn't be robbed.

"DISEASE, CRIME, THE POLICE AND POVERTY ARE THE CONSTANT COMPANIONS OF THE PEOPLE IN THE TOWNSHIPS."

Blacks who didn't work in the mines didn't fare much better. By day, blacks and whites crowded into bustling downtown Johannesburg. But night-time told a different story. As darkness fell, whites retreated to the safety and comfort of the suburbs. Blacks returned to their townships.

Townships are areas near a city – sprawling slums with row upon row of tiny, boxlike houses. Families often sleep three and four to a room, sometimes more. There is usually no running water, electricity or sanitary facilities. Disease, crime, the police and poverty are the constant companions of the people in the townships.

When Mandela arrived, the City of Gold was experiencing a surge in population. Many who came were not only seeking work in the mines. Many, like Mandela, were educated, ambitious and becoming more politically aware every day. They were frustrated by the world of legalized racism with which they were being forced to cope.

Each week Mandela struggled to set aside enough money to pay the rent. Sometimes he wasn't even sure if he would have bus fare. Fortunately, his landlord was sympathetic and allowed him at times to go without paying his rent.

After working briefly at Crown Mines, Nelson met Walter Sisulu.

Sisulu's father was white, but Walter, who had been raised by his mother, was dark-skinned. He was fired from his first job for insubordination. After that he had a number of jobs: in the mines and factories; at a bakery; and as a kitchen boy in a white household. At the bakery he organized the workers and was again fired. Not long after, Sisulu was sent to jail for fighting with a white ticket collector who he believed was abusing a black railway passenger. Later he opened an estate agency in Johannesburg and made a living selling what little land blacks could still purchase.

Mandela and Sisulu became good friends. When Mandela received his BA degree in 1942, Sisulu lent him money to buy a suit for his graduation ceremony. When Sisulu suggested that Mandela move in with him and his mother, he gratefully accepted.

Walter Sisulu had earned his reputation for being kind-hearted. No matter how little he had, he always had enough to help a friend in need. And Nelson Mandela was a friend and neighbour in need.

Walter Sisulu addressing a crowd in Johannesburg, 1989.

One thing the older Sisulu could give him was advice. A
job was another. Mandela was studying for his law degree,
and Sisulu introduced him to a senior partner in a white
Johannesburg law firm. Some white South African law firms
hired blacks as clerks. Mandela happily took the job.

In 1939, World War II had begun. Sisulu worked to convince black South Africans not to enlist in the army. Many
agreed with him. Why should they die helping to end racism
in a foreign land? Weren't they being treated just as badly by
their own racist government? The South African government
would not even allow blacks to carry weapons. They could
serve as stretcher bearers and drive vehicles and, if necessary, die doing that. But they couldn't shoot whites, even
those who were the enemy.

But many blacks disagreed with Sisulu's arguments. They hoped that by supporting the war effort and remaining loyal to the government they would be rewarded with better treatment when victory came. Thousands of black South Africans volunteered for military service during the war. And they saw what life was like in countries that didn't treat blacks as second-class citizens.

The Sisulus had many friends, and the atmosphere in their home was cheerful and warm. One of the guests was Sisulu's cousin, Evelyn Ntoko Mase. She was a nurse who had come to Johannesburg about the same time as Mandela. A month after their first meeting he proposed and, in 1944, they were married. That same year, Nelson Mandela joined the ANC, the African National Congress, which was to become increasingly important to him.

The Mandelas' first home was a very small two-room house in Orlando East, one of the townships outside Johannesburg. A year later their first son was born, and three more children followed shortly after.

Always athletic, Nelson continued to work hard keeping physically fit and eating right. He had been training to be a heavyweight boxer. Now he got up at dawn so he could jog a few miles before heading to the city.

Mandela tried to spend as much time as possible with his family. He played with the children and took them to local boxing tournaments. He also told them the stories he had heard as a child about the old days and how the trouble started between the blacks and the whites. He hoped this would help them understand why he spent so much time away from home.

For as much as he cared for his family, political activity came first.

In the early 1950s, Nelson Mandela's political activity kept him away from home more and more, often for days at a time. By 1955, he was absent so much that it was affecting his marriage. Two years later, he and Evelyn were divorced.

Five years earlier, in 1952, Mandela and Oliver Tambo had opened their own law practice in Johannesburg. It was the first black law partnership in South Africa. Mandela had known Tambo when they were students at Fort Hare College. Tambo had come to Johannesburg to teach maths and science but had decided to switch to law and practise with Mandela. They worked well together and enjoyed the many hours they spent arguing about politics and jazz, and eating hot Indian food.

They had no difficulty finding clients. Each morning, people waited patiently, sometimes overflowing into the corridors. Their problems ranged from the serious to the petty. From criminal offences to brewing beer illegally.

Mandela and Oliver Tambo also had their own problems with South Africa's race prejudice. Unlike white lawyers, they had to apply for permission to open an office in the city – permission that was never granted. They were told they had to work in the township where they lived. They decided to keep their office anyway, knowing that they were risking eviction or worse.

In 1962, law partners Oliver Tambo and Nelson Mandela (right) visited Addis Ababa, Ethiopia, together.

Day after day, with case after case, they were reminded of the misery brought about by the South African government's policy of separation of the races. Each client, each court appearance, each trial brought the situation into sharper focus.

Mandela's decision to become a member of the African National Congress strengthened his commitment to political action. Soon it was more important than anything else. Soon there was no time for anything but the African National Congress and its growing conflict with Afrikaners and apartheid.

PART 2: AFRIKANERS AND APARTHEID

3

THE BOERS
AND THE BRITISH

Africa, the world's second largest continent, is three times larger than Europe. It covers about one fifth of the land surface of the Earth. The world's largest desert, the Sahara (by itself almost as large as the United States), and the longest river, the Nile, are found in Africa. It is the home of thousands of different mammals, reptiles, fish and birds. The terrain varies from grasslands and mountain ranges to tropical rainforests.

Scholars consider Africa the birthplace of the human race. The earliest evidence of the existence of humans are fossils and bones that were discovered there.

In the 1400s and 1500s, European colonial powers began establishing trading posts along the coast of Africa. In the 1600s, the Dutch, and in the 1700s, other European nations began to explore the interior of the great continent. Portugal, Spain, France, Germany, the Netherlands and Great Britain were all countries seeking to forcibly rule parts of Africa.

An illustration of black South Africans being captured by a European slave hunter.

They wanted to establish colonies in Africa, chiefly for economic reasons. They wanted land, cattle, diamonds, gold, cheap labour, and other valuable raw materials that could be found there. Also they wanted to develop markets for their own goods.

Soon after they arrived, the Europeans forced the natives into slavery and sold them in other parts of the world. Slaves and gold were Africa's two most valuable exports. By the mid-1800s, ten million Africans had been forced into slavery.

Before the white man arrived, African tribes lived in the eastern half of South Africa. The Zulu, Xhosa, Sotho and other tribes farmed the land, tended cattle and hunted for food. They had their own religious beliefs, which were very different from Europe's Christian religions.

African tribes resisted colonial rule from the beginning. In South Africa the Zulu, Xhosa, Venda, Tswana and

Sotho fought valiantly against the white invaders. They tried to defend themselves and protect their land, but their spears and shields were no match for the Europeans' guns. Increasingly, the original black inhabitants of Africa had their land taken from them. By the late 1800s, white Europeans had conquered nearly all of Africa.

In 1652, the Dutch East India Trading Company sent about ninety men to the southern tip of Africa to set up a kind of refreshment station for their ships. The ships would stop there on their journey from the Netherlands to the Far East and on the return trip. This settlement became known as the Cape Colony.

Soon immigrants from Europe arrived to begin a new life. They considered themselves pioneers settling a primitive continent. They began to farm the land, eventually using the cheap labour of the black natives. By the 1700s, there were more slaves than white settlers.

In 1806, Great Britain seized the area from the Dutch and began to impose their rule. The settlers, called *Boers*, a Dutch word meaning farmer, objected to much of British rule. The policy that caused the strongest reaction concerned slaves. Between 1834 and 1838, the British abolished slavery, including those slaves owned by the Boers.

Even the way the British offered financial compensation angered the Boers. They could receive about a third of the slaves' value but the money had to be picked up in London. Most who lived in the Cape Colony were unlikely to make the trip.

The Boers decided that they had had enough of British rule. They were determined to preserve their way of life. They refused to live in a society where whites were not the masters and blacks the servants. They believed that God had decided that whites should rule and blacks should serve.

In 1836, they began gathering their sheep, cattle and slaves and, loading their ox-drawn wagons with their belongings, they started what became known as The Great Trek. In the first two years, approximately six thousand men, women and children headed hundreds of miles into the treacherous interior of the continent. Piet Retief, one of their leaders, explained their decision: they hoped the British government would "allow us to govern ourselves ... in the future ... we are resolved, wherever we go, that we will uphold the just principles of liberty; but ... it is our determination to maintain ... and preserve proper relations between master and servant."

Many died along the way. Some of disease, some of hunger and some from exhaustion. Others died during the violent confrontations with the Zulu, the Xhosa and other African tribes who lived along their route. One famous encounter is known as the Battle of Blood River.

The battle occurred because the Boers felt they had been deceived by a Zulu chief who had agreed to give them land.

Zulu means 'the heavens', and the Zulu are the 'people of the heavens'. The Zulu kingdom had been greatly expanded by Shaka, their most famous leader. Shaka was a ruthless ruler with a genius for military tactics.

He drove his warriors to the edge. They could travel fifty miles a day, living off the land. Shaka made them run barefoot. When there were complaints, he made them dance on thorns spread on the ground. Those who stopped to comfort themselves were killed. Shaka created a new type of spear. It had a broad base and a short handle. This allowed his warriors to fight up close. He enlarged their shields, toughened them and colour-coded them by regiment. Zulu soldiers were not allowed to marry. They were disciplined troops.

Shaka could and would order someone killed for the slightest reason. His executioners obediently ended the life of a Zulu whose offence was as slight as sneezing while Shaka was eating. Instant death could result from displeasing him in any way.

Within three years, Shaka had increased Zulu territory from three hundred and fifty square miles to over ten thousand. His army now numbered twenty thousand. The Zulu kingdom was the mightiest in all of black South Africa.

The Boers, continuing their search for farmland and independence, were nearing Zulu territory. Shaka had been killed and replaced by his half brother Dingane. Although Dingane was nowhere near as brilliant a general as Shaka, he was just as ruthless. The Zulu nation was the most powerful the Boers had yet encountered.

Piet Retief requested permission from Dingane to settle on uninhabited Zulu land. In October 1837, Retief met with Dingane. The Zulu leader agreed to allow the Boers to settle on the land.

When news of the agreement reached the Boer camp, they prepared to move. Thousands of wagons began rumbling over the land. But Dingane had been suspicious of the Boers from the beginning. It had been prophesied that there would be an invasion: perhaps this was it? Dingane would take no chances. The Boers, having defeated all they encountered so far, proceeded with little fear.

Dingane invited Retief and his party to celebrate the agreement. The Boers left their guns behind. When the celebration was at its height, Dingane gave the order for the Boers to be killed.

The following morning – at dawn – three Zulu regiments attacked the Boer families, which were camped nearby. Forty-one men, fifty-six women and one hundred and eighty-five children were killed.

Shaken, but not willing to turn back, the Boers swore revenge. Within a year, they were reinforced and ready. Before the attack the Boers asked God to help them triumph over the enemy. They vowed to observe that day as a day of thanksgiving. On December 16, 1838, that day came.

Four hundred and sixty-four Boers confronted an estimated twelve thousand Zulus. The Boers, however, had positioned themselves brilliantly. The Zulus' numerical superiority acted against them. They found themselves hemmed in by the banks of the river bordering the Boer position. There were so many and so little room that their six-foot steel-tipped throwing spears were of little use. The clusters of Zulus made easy targets for the sharpshooting Boers barricaded behind their circled wagons. No Zulu reached a Boer wagon. Hundreds, many wounded and dying, fell into the river, which ran red with their blood. Groups of Boers tracked down and shot those who tried to flee. When their bullets ran out, they used pebbles.

Over three thousand Zulus died and not one Boer.

They'd had their revenge.

For the Boers their victory was a sign that God was on their side. To them it was also a sign that black people could not be trusted.

The Great Trek lasted from 1836 to 1854. By the time it was over, the Boers had established two independent republics: the Transvaal and the Orange Free State.

The Boers thought The Great Trek had taken them far enough to escape the British, but it hadn't. After the discovery of diamonds and gold in the late 1800s, British

English soldiers in the Boer War.

interest in the area increased. The diamond and gold discoveries caused tremendous changes. Industry blossomed the economy boomed, and the population grew. Skilled and unskilled workers came seeking jobs and opportunity. Great Britain took steps to insure that the two new republics the Boers had established remained within British colonial rule.

The Boers decided to fight for their independence, and, in 1899, the Boer War began. The fifty thousand Boer farmers were badly outnumbered, but they surprised the British. Using guerilla tactics (hit-and-run actions, disappearing into the countryside), they scored a series of early victories. The British had assumed the war would be over in a matter of weeks – a month or two at most. But now they had to send more troops into the area, eventually totalling over four hundred thousand men.

They burned the Boers' farms and killed millions of their cattle, sheep and horses. One hundred and fifty thousand civilians were forced into concentration camps. Disease broke out in the overcrowded camps, and twenty-six thousand, mostly women and children, died.

The Boers were unable to hold out against the might of the British Empire. By June 1900, the British had captured Pretoria, the capital of the Transvaal. Finally, in 1902, the Boers admitted defeat.

4
AFRIKANERS
AND APARTHEID

The Boers had lost the war but won the peace. Nearly a decade later, in 1910, the Union of South Africa was declared an independent state within the British Empire. The new constitution gave all power to the whites. And the new government began making sure almost immediately that black Africans remained oppressed, exploited and, most importantly, separated from whites. A series of laws were passed monitoring every move and removing every right. In the coming years, life for blacks in South Africa worsened.

Blacks were no longer allowed to own land. Almost ninety per cent of South Africa was designated for whites only. Even though blacks outnumbered whites, they were required to live on land totalling less than ten per cent of the country. Unable to live off the land, they continued to flow into the ever-expanding cities in search of jobs.

But they were not allowed to live *in* the cities. Cities

"BLACKS WERE NO LONGER ALLOWED TO OWN LAND. ALMOST NINETY PER CENT OF SOUTH AFRICA WAS DESIGNATED FOR WHITES ONLY."

were reserved for whites. Blacks were required to live in areas set aside for them near the cities – the townships.

The few blacks who had managed to buy land before 1910 were forced to leave. They were resettled in the homelands, rural areas reserved for black South Africans.

Homelands, the government explained, were places where blacks could live grouped by tribe, as they had lived in the past. It had been, however, many generations since most blacks had lived like that. To most, the homelands were just miserably overcrowded places. They were unable to support the large number of people forced to live there.

The best and best-paying jobs were reserved for whites, while blacks continued to do the jobs that paid very little.

Blacks were not allowed to form political parties, had no representation in government and could not vote.

In 1931, Great Britain granted the Union of South Africa full independence. Seventeen years later, in 1948, the National Party led by D. F. Malan won a narrow victory in the general election. The victory was significant. The Afrikaners had taken over the reins of political power. *Afrikaner* (af-rih-KAHN-er) is a Dutch word meaning African. The Afrikaners were the direct descendants of the original Dutch, German and French settlers: the Boers. They spoke Afrikaans (af-rih-KAHNZ), a language derived from Dutch. They had been poor, the poorest of the whites in South Africa. They worked mostly in unskilled jobs, and a third of the Afrikaners farmed the land. They were aware that blacks were becoming more skilled, and they feared that soon they would be competing with them for jobs. The government had been, they felt, far too liberal. The black African had to be put down and kept down. If he wasn't, there would be trouble. The white British immigrants who had come in increasing numbers over the years had most of the money, but now the Afrikaners had the power.

The National Party instituted more than a hundred laws aimed at keeping blacks and whites separate... and unequal. This was the beginning of a radical political philosophy of racial segregation called *apartheid* (ah-PAHRT-hayt). Apartheid means separateness in Afrikaans and, as of 1948, it was the official policy of the South African government.

One law, the Population Registration Act, was an attempt

A Johannesburg resident displays the passbook that all blacks had to carry with them.

to ensure (in the view of the National Party) the purity of the white race. Race inspectors examined skin, hair and nails to determine a person's proper racial classification. They inspected babies in hospitals and investigated when someone's race was in question. One joke had it, "They put a pencil in your hair – if it falls out you're white, if it stays in you're coloured".

The laws required that blacks carry identification papers at all times, anywhere they went. These passbooks allowed the government to control where blacks lived and worked. Pass laws were among the most hated of the apartheid laws. Passbooks had to be produced on demand. They could be issued by any white person, even children. The pass laws were vigorously enforced. On average, two hundred thousand Africans a year were arrested for violations. If and when their cases came to trial, their guilt or innocence was often determined in minutes, sometimes seconds. In the case of a guilty verdict there could be fines, jail or banishment to one of the homelands. Thousands were convicted of pass law violations every year.

The laws also said people could be detained without trial. Blacks were frequently placed in solitary confinement without being charged with any crime.

Until 1980, even zoos were segregated, as were the beaches. White couples were given money by the government if they got married, and even more if they had children; black couples were not. There were white ambulances and black ambulances.

By the mid-1950s, the National Party was all-powerful. It had made good on its promise to keep blacks in their place. Blacks in South Africa were deprived of their land, their homes and their freedom of movement. They could do very little to better themselves. Even if they were qualified for a better job, in most cases it was against the law to give it to them. Their hopes of being treated as equal members of South African society were gone.

The Afrikaners had come a long way since 1910. Now, over forty years later, apartheid was the law of the land. At last they were living in the society their ancestors had dreamed of and died for: a society where whites were the masters.

PART 3:
THE STRUGGLE

5
THE AFRICAN
NATIONAL CONGRESS

In 1912, two years after the formation of the Union of South Africa, another union was formed. A conference of black leaders was convened to urge black South Africans to unite for the struggle against the new, white, Afrikaner government.

One of the conference leaders addressed the gathering:

Chiefs of royal blood and gentlemen of our race, we have gathered together to consider and discuss a scheme which my colleagues and I have decided to place before you. We have discovered that in the land of their birth, Africans are treated as hewers of wood and drawers of water. The white people of this country have formed what is known as the Union of South Africa – a union in which we have no voice in the making of the laws and no part in the administration.

They hoped to put aside problems between tribes and concentrate on the one problem that plagued them all: apartheid. Unless they were able to put an end to apartheid, black South Africans would be condemned to lives dominated by the white minority.

The black leaders came from widely different backgrounds. Some were tribal chiefs, and some were clerks. There were businessmen, political leaders, clergymen and lawyers. Geographically they represented all parts of South Africa: the cities and the rural areas, the coasts and the interior, and they spoke a number of different languages and dialects.

The conference opened with the hymn *'Nkosi Sikelel' iAfrika'* ('God Bless Africa'). This became the anthem of the new African National Congress. The ANC intended to call attention to the practice of racial segregation in South Africa: in the administration of government laws, and in education, jobs, housing and living conditions. They planned to use peaceful methods. It would be a multiracial organization: the founding members of the ANC believed that racism was evil, and they invited all, regardless of colour, to join. Their goal was racial harmony.

The ANC would strive to provide a unified voice that represented the black majority in South Africa.

In 1919, the ANC organized its first public action. Thousands demonstrated outside the central pass office in Johannesburg. They intended to hand in their papers as a protest against the pass laws. But before they could do so

A sign indicating that even the beach is a white-only area, 1976.

the police charged the crowd and arrested seven hundred demonstrators.

Over the next decade, the ANC arranged meetings, organized protests and staged demonstrations. All were nonviolent, and all resulted in increased repression and use of force by the police.

The ANC was led by patient men. The leadership felt that the best course of action would be to point out the injustices of apartheid so that whites would come to see its evils. Then they would vote to remove the oppressive laws. They looked to some whites as potential allies. But after twenty years, the ANC had little to show for its patience.

By the 1930s, the organization had fallen into decline. There was too much talk and too little action. The membership, once exuberant, had grown apathetic.

By the mid-1940s, many younger members of the ANC had tired of waiting for whites to help. They felt more forceful steps were necessary. Intelligent and impatient, they had grown defiant. Their influence was about to cause significant changes in the political philosophy of the African National Congress.

More than anything the change was one of perspective. To belong to the ANC all you had to do was be against apartheid – this would not change. But Africans knew that they were in fact the original inhabitants of the continent: this was *their* country. They wanted full citizenship, and they wanted to take a more active role in the leadership of the ANC. Many young ANC members contributed to this change, but none more than Nelson Mandela.

6

THE YOUTH LEAGUE

Nelson Mandela considered himself a loyal member of the ANC. It represented the best hope for a united stand against apartheid. But he agreed with much of the criticism. The ANC *had* grown weak. The leadership *had* become cautious and had compromised when they should have confronted. They had cared too much about the support of liberal white South Africans. To maintain this support they had acted with moderation – too much moderation.

The ANC had to demonstrate that they could boldly lead black South Africans out of the misery and poverty that threatened to engulf them. They had to demonstrate to their followers that they were capable of leading them into the future.

The idea developed of creating a separate division of the African National Congress. This would satisfy those who wanted change as well as those who wanted to work within the ANC. The organization's leadership could see that the repressive policies of the Afrikaner government demanded that they remain strong. To do that they had to remain unified while recognizing the need for change.

Mandela, Sisulu, Tambo and sixty others founded the Youth League of the African National Congress and began lengthy discussions defining their political philosophy.

One controversy concerned their relationship with South African whites. Some believed that whites must leave Africa. Africa belonged to the black people. *They* were the rightful rulers of a continent that had been forcibly divided and conquered by white European colonialists. Black Africans must not give up until they "drove the white man into the sea", as some put it.

Mandela disagreed with this approach. For one thing, it was unrealistic. The different racial groups in South Africa – black, white, coloured and Asian – had come to stay. Although Mandela felt that whites had to be convinced to end their domination of Africans, he also believed that South Africa must become a society free of any kind of racism. Whites, the League decided, were not necessarily friend or foe. What mattered was that blacks had to take responsibility for their own future.

Created in 1944, the Youth League forced the ANC, by the end of the decade, to become more of a mass movement. The time was right. As South Africa's industry grew and foreign investment increased, the whites were becoming richer and the blacks poorer. Hundreds of thousands of Africans were being crammed into the already overcrowded townships that were spreading near the country's cities. Urban blacks suffered unemployment, ill health,

Overcrowding in the townships caused squatter camps to spring up, like this one near Johannesburg where more than 50,000 blacks lived in shanties.

forced removal from their homes, constant police pressure and worse – much worse. As living conditions in the townships deteriorated, blacks became more aggressive.

The new Youth League had to take action. They wanted to involve as many people as possible. Petitions, discussions and polite letters of protest would no longer be enough. New methods of resistance – nonviolent, but outside the legal framework – had to be employed. There would be boycotts, mass demonstrations and other forms of civil disobedience. The African National Congress was about to become more militant.

When Nelson Mandela first joined in the founding of the ANC Youth League, he participated vigorously in establishing its philosophy. But he rarely spoke at the various larger meetings and conferences. Three years later, in 1947, this changed when he was elected secretary. He began to become known to the members as well as to the public. He continued, however, to be friendly and modest in spite of his growing popularity.

In 1951, he was elected president of the Youth League.

7
THE DEFIANCE CAMPAIGN

In 1952, the African National Congress acted. The ANC organized South Africa's first nationwide protest against apartheid. The year before, the ANC had met and called for the repeal of six particularly unjust laws. The meeting lasted for three days. Mandela, Sisulu and other members of the Youth League proposed that it was time to confront the government.

A letter was sent to Prime Minister Malan. It explained that for many years the ANC had used proper constitutional channels to voice its protests. But these protests had fallen on deaf ears. The government had not responded to a single request. In fact, each request was followed by increased persecution. They had been left no choice. Unless the government repealed the six unjust laws by April 6, 1952, a campaign of defiance would begin.

The action was enthusiastically approved. Volunteers would be organized to defy the oppressive laws. It came to be called the Defiance Campaign, and it was launched in June.

It was the boldest step in the nearly forty-year history of the ANC.

This time the government did reply. No, they would not repeal the laws, and any subversive activities would be dealt with swiftly and severely.

Nelson Mandela was given responsibility for all volunteer activity, including coordinating ANC branches and raising funds.

He travelled to every part of South Africa. Travel itself was often a problem. Trains ran infrequently, blacks were not allowed in most hotels and taxis wouldn't pick them up. Many times they were forced to walk from house to house, with no assurance that they would be welcome when they arrived.

When they were welcome, Mandela patiently explained the plan, sometimes staying into the night. He spoke to handfuls of people or thousands in workers' halls. His confidence inspired people. He convinced them that they could do something about oppression. But he warned them that the government would try to intimidate them – especially those who were the first to defy the laws. He taught that they must not retaliate, no matter what the provocation. They must restrain themselves in the face of verbal and physical abuse. Discipline must rule. Volunteers had to be well behaved, dignified, and in control of their anger – something, he confessed, he had had difficulty with

"NONVIOLENCE, MANDELA EXPLAINED, OFTEN SHOWED MORE COURAGE THAN VIOLENCE."

in the past. But, he assured them, it *could* be done. Indeed, it *had* to be done; nonviolence was their only alternative. The government was heavily armed and would use force ruthlessly if given an excuse. They must not give them that excuse. Nonviolence, Mandela explained, often showed more courage than violence.

Mandela recruited 8,577 volunteers. Some wore armbands with the green, gold and black colours of the ANC flag. Black for the people, green for the land and gold for the resources.

They set out peacefully to use the whites-only entrances to railway stations, waiting rooms and post offices. They ignored curfews, entered areas that were forbidden and refused to present their passbooks. Over the next six months, thousands went to jail in a successful demonstration of orderly, mass, passive resistance. Their behaviour earned them admiration from abroad. The United Nations established a commission to inquire into apartheid. The fact that apartheid was being questioned formally by those outside South Africa encouraged Mandela and the ANC leadership.

But the government could not allow the campaign to continue – they began to crack down. Two more laws made it illegal to encourage blacks to resist the law. Disobedience could be punished by lashing, among other things.

Police activity increased. The mere holding of a meeting was outlawed, and pass laws were enforced even more strictly. Rioting, which some believed was caused by undercover government agents to justify further use of force, broke out.

Hundred of blacks were shot and killed by the police, and thousands more were wounded. Police raided homes across the country and arrested black leaders, including Mandela. The campaign began to lose its momentum and soon ceased.

The Defiance Campaign had failed to achieve its major goals. Civil disobedience had not worked. None of the laws had been repealed. The ANC, committed throughout its history to nonviolence, had not been able to effectively counter government violence. Mandela, and practically every other organizer of the campaign, was banned. A banning order was issued by the government. It prevented someone from doing any or all of the following:

- attending any gathering specified by the government
- entering an educational institution
- entering an airport
- entering the offices of a newspaper or magazine or being quoted in one
- writing anything for publication
- leaving the district to which he or she had been confined
- belonging to any organization specified by the government

Banning orders might, and often did, require the banned person to report once a week to the police and to remain at home during certain hours.

A banning order could be issued without proof; it was not even necessary to bring charges. Banned people could not even communicate with one another.

However, despite the defeats, much had been gained.

The Defiance Campaign was a landmark event in the history of the African National Congress. Its membership had grown from a few thousand to a hundred thousand. Black South Africans saw that they did not have to simply give in to government oppression. The campaign gave them a sense of dignity. Thousands of the participants had learned new political principles, and the leadership had learned lessons as well. They had to be willing to sacrifice and, if necessary, face imprisonment. They also had to be prepared to die for the principles they believed in.

For Nelson Mandela, it was his first experience with real political action. It was also the first time he had been arrested and banned.

The struggle had begun.

8

THE FREEDOM CHARTER AND THE TREASON TRIAL

In 1953, the ANC, working with other groups, proposed a Congress of the People. The purpose of the Congress was to agree on a bill of rights for all South Africans, regardless of race. This manifesto was called the Freedom Charter.

The Freedom Charter would define the future democratic South Africa that most blacks had hoped to see. The Congress of the People would summon representatives from all parts of the country.

That same year the National Party had been elected for a second term. The number of oppressive laws was increasing. The Afrikaners had recently ruled that schools run by missionaries would be placed under government control. Mission schools had been the only places blacks could get a Western education. The law caused widespread anger. Pass laws were being enforced vigorously, and police harassment was becoming part of the daily existence of many black South Africans.

Mandela, Sisulu and others began preparing for the Congress. A national council was formed to mobilize the people. They were contacted to find out what their concerns were – not only their complaints but their ideas for the future. People were contacted in a variety of ways, some via the ANC newspaper *New Age*. Some villages received circulars asking, "If you could make the laws ... what would you do?" or "How would you set about making South Africa a happy place to be?" Some were canvassed at meetings, which had to be conducted in secret because of the banning orders that applied to Mandela and others. Mandela was now president of the Transvaal branch of the ANC. At the annual conference someone else read his presidential address so that he wouldn't be arrested on the spot.

The responses began coming in. Some spoke of immediate needs: farming assistance, higher wages, better housing, food and education. Others spoke about a society free of oppression.

The preparations for the mass gatherings took over a year. Millions of responses were considered. A committee sifted through the responses, and a draft of the Freedom Charter was written. When it was approved by Mandela and others, it was ready to be presented to the Congress of the People.

On Sunday, June 26, 1955, they made their way from all over South Africa to a football field ten miles outside of Johannesburg. The roads leading to the City of Gold were crowded with delegates. Many travelled by bus or truck, their blankets and food piled beside them. The

Some of the 2,884 delegates who arrived at the Congress of the People on June 26, 1955.

joyous mood was not dampened by the police roadblocks that slowed their progress.

It was the most representative gathering in the history of South Africa. Although the majority were blacks, there were many whites. There were doctors, lawyers, servants, students, teachers, city workers and housewives. Ministers marched next to labourers and peasants. Many held banners. FREEDOM IN OUR LIVES; LONG LIVE THE STRUGGLE, read two. There were 2,884 delegates and hundreds of spectators. Mandela, again because of his banning order, was disguised, watching from a distance. The colours of the ANC were everywhere.

On the platform stood a giant four-spoked white wheel symbolizing the unity of the Congress.

The painstaking process of ratifying the Freedom Charter began. It was read aloud in English, Xhosa and Zulu. Each paragraph was debated with the delegates speaking for the people they represented.

The Freedom Charter began:

We, the people of South Africa, declare for all our country and the world to know:

- *that South Africa belongs to all who live in it, black and white, and that no government can justly claim authority unless it is based on the will of all the people*
- *that our people have been robbed of their birthright to land, liberty and peace by a form of government founded on injustice and inequality*
- *that our country will never be prosperous or free until all our people live in brotherhood, enjoying equal rights and opportunities*
- *that only a democratic state, based on the will of all the people, can secure to all their birthright without distinction of colour, race, sex, or belief.*

The government had been invited to attend but sent instead a battalion of police. In the afternoon, armed with tanks and Sten guns, they raided the Congress. They announced over the microphone that no one would be allowed to leave. Every document they could find was seized. All entrances were blocked, and the delegates were searched one by one. The questioning went on into the night.

The following year, on December 5, 1956, Nelson Mandela and nearly the entire ANC leadership were arrested in a massive sweep operation. Anyone associated with the Freedom Charter was taken into custody.

The government said the Freedom Charter was a blueprint for violent revolution and those responsible for it were guilty of treason. The police raided the homes and offices of hundreds of men and women. They seized letters, diaries – anything that might be evidence of treason. The raids continued throughout the year and were the biggest in South African history.

Those arrested represented a cross section of South African society. Most were workers: clerks, teachers, drivers, etc. They were taken, some by military aircraft, to the prison in Johannesburg. There were one hundred and fifty-six prisoners, men and women of all races, and they all would stand trial for high treason.

When the Treason Trial began on December 19, 1956, all one hundred and fifty-six defendants sat together, row after row. On the first day, the microphone was not working, and court had to be adjourned. When court reconvened the next day, the defendants had been placed behind a six-foot-high wire barrier. The defence objected to their clients being treated like animals. The cages were removed and bail was granted. In spite of the seriousness of the charges, the atmosphere was hopeful. Mandela's banning orders had kept him separated from his colleagues. Now, kept in two enormous cells, they were able to compare notes and make plans.

The trial dragged on for an incredible four and a half years, until 1961. It was a trying and tiring trial. In the first month alone, twelve thousand documents were entered against the accused. (Today, the documents presented at the Treason Trial fill twenty-eight reels of microfilm.)

Besides the defendants themselves, the Freedom

TREASON TRIAL

The ACCUSED

DECEMBE 1956

The 156 defendants in the Treason Trial; Nelson Mandela, in the third row from the bottom at the centre, stands out because of his height.

Charter itself was on trial. The length of the trial was also a problem. South Africa's black leadership was unable to concentrate on anything else for four long years.

Many of the defendants lost their jobs or had to close their businesses because they were away for so long. As the months turned into years, the efforts of the defence resulted in a victory. The cases against most of the accused were dropped. At the end only thirty, including Mandela, remained to face charges.

From the beginning, international attention was focused on the Treason Trial. Money for legal expenses was collected by a defence committee. Representatives from European judicial organizations came to South Africa to witness and report on the proceedings. The defendants were represented by highly capable lawyers who were able, at times, to make the prosecution look foolish. The state's presentation of its case was uncoordinated and the testimony of witnesses often unconvincing.

Mandela's lengthy testimony (four hundred and forty-one pages of court record) was measured and eloquent.

In our experience the most important thing about imperialism today is that it has gone all over the world subjugating people and exploiting them, bringing death and destruction to millions of people. That is the central thing, and we want to know whether we should support and perpetuate this institution which has brought so much suffering.

During the Treason Trial, the crowd cheered in support of the accused as they were driven away from court.

His explanation of the ANC policies and his composure and good humour throughout brought him and the organization worldwide respect.

At last, in late March 1961, Mandela and his twenty-nine co-defendants heard the verdict. It was a sombre moment: they could receive the death penalty. The judge said that the state had failed to prove its case.

On all the evidence presented to this court and in our finding of fact it is impossible to ... come to the conclusion that the ANC had acquired or adopted a policy to overthrow the state by violence.

All had been acquitted and were discharged.

9
NOMZAMO WINIFRED MADIKIZELA

Since 1952, when he and Oliver Tambo first opened their law practice, Nelson Mandela's private life had begun to disappear.

After solving the difficulties of finding an office in whites-only downtown Johannesburg, the practice flourished. As its reputation grew, so did their list of clients. Their office became a centre of political activity. During the Treason Trial, Mandela and Tambo tried to keep the practice going, but their time was consumed by the trial.

Mandela's personal reputation as a lawyer and political activist was also growing. His refusal to obey apartheid laws won him the admiration of many blacks. He was handsome and dignified. His intelligence, eloquence and bold presence in the courtroom distinguished him. Whenever he was scheduled to plead a case, there were more spectators than usual.

But the combination of his political activities and his legal responsibilities left little room for anything else. His marriage, unable to survive these burdens, had ended in divorce. But during the Treason Trial, he met Nomzamo Winifred Madikizela.

Nomzamo means 'she who strives', and it certainly fit. But she had been called Winnie since her baptism as a Methodist. Born on September 26, 1936, Winnie was the fifth of nine children. She was raised in the same village as Oliver Tambo: a remote, backward area that sat between the mountains and the sea. She grew up a barefoot peasant girl.

Like Mandela, when Winnie was a child, she helped tend the cattle and the sheep, plough the land and milk the cows. Every day, balancing a drum on her head, she fetched water from a little stream.

Also like Mandela, she grew up listening to her elders tell her of the injustices suffered by blacks at the hands of whites. Her grandmother taught her the meaning of the African saying, 'When the white people came we had the land and they had the Bible. Now we have the Bible and they have the land'.

Winnie's father also told her how the whites stole their cattle and destroyed their way of life.

Although her family had little money or material wealth, they were better educated than most. Both her parents were teachers. Winnie grew up with a love of reading and was always at the top of her class.

Rather than accept an arranged marriage, she, too, had left home. She went to Johannesburg to study social work.

After Nelson Mandela and Winnie Madikizela met, they saw each other almost every day.

She did so well that she won a scholarship to study at a university in the United States. But she decided that her own country came first. She became the first black medical social worker in South Africa.

Winnie had seen Mandela once in court. The people around her whispered his name when he walked in.

One of Winnie's friends who was a nurse was soon to marry Oliver Tambo. The three of them ran into Mandela one day. During an adjournment in the trial, he called her and invited her to lunch. Winnie was nervous because Mandela was already a well-known name.

Mandela loved hot, curried Indian food. Winnie, who had never eaten curry, soon had a severe case of watery eyes because of the spices. And that wasn't the only problem. Their conversation was constantly interrupted by people coming to the table to consult him or to get his advice.

But they saw each other almost every day after that. Even then, though, their time together was limited. When he called for her, he had his sports clothes on. He was usually on his way to work out. It wasn't long before he had to run off to another day of meetings.

Winnie could see how dedicated he was to the struggle for liberation. But Nelson Mandela's commitment suited Winnie more than it might have suited others. She herself was seriously involved with her social work.

Mandela never came right out and proposed. One day in late March 1957, he mentioned a dressmaker who could make her wedding gown. He wasn't being arrogant; it was just understood that they would be married. Winnie was very happy about the idea of marrying Nelson Mandela.

They talked honestly about the difficulties of their new relationship. If he was found guilty at the Treason Trial, he was likely to go to prison for a long time. Even if he wasn't, his life was bound to be one of constant scrutiny by the police. He wanted to be sure she understood that his commitment to freedom was for life.

Winnie understood that being with Nelson was different from anything she had experienced. She could not think that their marriage would be like others. For Nelson

Mandela, South Africa came first; everything else would have to wait. Winnie wouldn't have it any other way.

Winnie's father and stepmother (her mother died when she was nine) were not certain she was making the right decision. They were worried about the kind of life she would be starting with someone as politically active as Mandela.

The couple, however, *were* sure, and the marriage plans went forward. Mandela paid the *lobola* that is traditional in African weddings. *Lobola* is the price paid by the bridegroom to the bride's father. It was usually paid with cattle, and the long, involved bargaining process was part of the enjoyment. The bride is never told how many cattle she was thought to be worth (and to this day Winnie doesn't know).

The banned husband-to-be applied for permission to leave Johannesburg to attend his own wedding. Permission was granted on the condition that he conduct no other business.

They were married on June 14, 1958, near the village where Winnie was born and raised.

Mandela, however, had to get back to Johannesburg and the trial. The ceremony had not even been completed in the traditional manner. They were supposed to be married in his home also, but they didn't have time. Winnie kept part of the wedding cake for the completion of the ceremony.

Back in Johannesburg, Winnie Mandela set about making their house a home. She always had a flair for colour

Nelson and Winnie Mandela on their wedding day, June 14, 1958.

and style, and she brought both to the modest two-room brick house. It was located in the township of Soweto. They were fortunate to have some things that few in Soweto had: electricity, hot water and an indoor bathroom.

Mandela's children from his first marriage visited them on weekends. And he and Winnie began their own family: two daughters – Zeni, born in 1959, and Zindzi, in 1960.

As expected, their home life was nowhere near normal. Nelson woke as early as four A.M. to run. The streets were usually empty. People had not yet begun to make their way to the buses that would take them on the long journey to the mines and factories. After his run he had fresh orange juice, a raw egg and toast. Then he left for Pretoria, where the trial was being held. Often he stayed overnight preparing his defence.

Weekends were taken up with other court cases or ANC business. He was rarely home an entire weekend. Even when he was, he wasn't alone. More often than not, he would surprise Winnie with friends. Somehow she managed to make sure there was dinner for everyone. She even began to get something of a reputation for her hot curry dishes.

By the end of the 1950s, Mandela's law practice had deteriorated. But Nelson Mandela was, in a sense, no longer a lawyer. He had become the leader of his people.

10

THE SHARPEVILLE MASSACRE

By 1960, the Afrikaners had controlled the government of South Africa for twelve years. During that time, they continued to pass laws that strengthened apartheid.

They took steps to ensure that blacks eventually would not become citizens of South Africa. Afrikaners believed that Africans should be made to live grouped together by tribe. Thirteen per cent of the land in South Africa was set aside for eight tribal homelands. These homelands were rural reserves where millions of blacks would now be forced to live. There, according to the government, they could develop properly among their own people. They could advance in the homelands, unlike in white South Africa, where advancement was impossible. Black South Africans would still be allowed to work in the eighty-seven per cent of the country that was reserved for whites. They would even be able to travel there, provided they had the proper identification. But they would be considered immigrants, people from a foreign country. Eventually, according to the plan, the homelands would be granted independence as nations.

Millions of blacks were to be uprooted and forced to live in rural slums. Areas that were overcrowded would now be forced to support an even larger population. To black leaders, this policy was designed to keep blacks further divided and prevent them from uniting against the government.

Afrikaner attitudes toward black education had also been clarified over the past decade. They said that allowing black children to receive the same education as whites created unrealistic expectations. This led to frustration and unrest. The curriculum for blacks was redesigned. Blacks could now be taught from an early age that they were inferior to whites, and that they had best accept their lowly status.

In the face of such oppression, many blacks questioned the ANC's nonviolent approach. Although they respected what the ANC stood for, they wondered how effective it had been. Although the ANC had been courageous on occasion, some felt they were falling behind the times. Young blacks, especially those who lived in the poverty-stricken and disease-ridden townships, needed an organization that spoke their language.

In 1959, Robert Sobukwe broke away from the ANC and established the Pan African Congress.

Sobukwe was born in the Cape Province in 1924, the last of six children. His father was a labourer, and Robert contributed to the family's income by chopping wood. He grew up a Methodist and, with financial help from missionaries, entered Fort Hare College in 1947. Within a year, he was one of the ANC Youth League's most active and outspoken members. He also became the head of the Fort Hare Student Representative Council.

After graduation he taught at a high school. He was fired for publicly defending the Defiance Campaign.

Unlike Nelson Mandela, however, Sobukwe never accepted white participation in the struggle to create a new, democratic South Africa. He disagreed strongly with the Freedom Charter's first clause: *South Africa belongs to all who live in it, black and white.* The PAC, unlike the ANC, did not accept white members.

An eloquent speaker, Sobukwe had explained his position in a speech given to his graduation class:

We have been accused of blood thirstiness because we preach 'noncollaboration'. I wish to state here tonight that that is the only choice open to us. History has taught us that a group in power has never voluntarily relinquished its position. It has always been forced to do so. And we do not expect miracles to happen in South Africa.

Sobukwe and his followers identified with African states to the north that had recently won their independence. These victories inspired the PAC leaders.

Like Mandela, however, Sobukwe did believe in a society

Robert Sobukwe broke away from the African National Congress and formed the Pan African Congress.

free of racial discrimination: a South Africa where colour would be irrelevant. But until racial equality was achieved, whites could not be considered part of the struggle.

Robert Sobukwe and the Pan African Congress urged blacks to shed their slave mentality and accept their true African personality. They had to stop accepting white mistreatment.

Their first major effort was directed at the pass laws. The ANC was set to launch their own campaign. The PAC, aware of the ANC plans, decided to act. They needed to show what they were capable of. Their members were pressuring them to act quickly. The PAC scheduled their campaign for March 21, 1960, ten days earlier than the

ANC's campaign. It was a date that was to become a turning point in the history of the black struggle in South Africa.

The PAC asked blacks to turn in their passbooks and allow themselves to be arrested. If enough people participated, the jails would become filled, and South African industry would be deprived of much-needed labour. Eventually, the PAC hoped, this strategy of mass arrests would force the government to abolish the pass laws.

Leaflets were distributed nationwide instructing residents to stay away from work and hand in their passbooks. Sobukwe had taken the precaution of contacting the commissioner of police. He told him that the protesters would be instructed to remain nonviolent. He requested that the commissioner ask his men to also show restraint.

In most areas protesters were arrested without incident, but not in Sharpeville.

The township of Sharpeville is fifty miles south of Johannesburg. It is located near the steel mills, where unemployment and rent increases plagued black workers. The people of Sharpeville responded to the PAC's call and began to assemble on the morning of March 21, 1960. Many in the crowd were simply curious residents.

Police estimated the crowd at twenty thousand. Others say it was closer to five thousand. Eyewitness accounts of the mood of the crowd also vary. Some describe it as well mannered and under control. But police witnesses say the demonstrators were armed with sticks and were hostile.

The police were heavily outnumbered and became nervous as the day wore on. When the crowd first arrived at the police station, there were only twelve police officers on hand. But by noon, two hundred reinforcements had arrived.

The demonstrators refused to disperse even when the planes buzzed them and they were sprayed with tear gas. Some say the crowd began to surge against the fence that enclosed the station, and then the fence began to sway. The police were ordered to line up facing the demonstrators. They tried to arrest three of the PAC leaders. When the gates were opened, the crowd attempted to come through the opening. The police were jittery, ready to snap. Some say the police attempted to push back the crowd; others say that they merely tried to hold them back.

Suddenly, two shots rang out, followed by twenty seconds of uninterrupted gunfire. Some of the crowd thought the police were firing blanks. Children who had been playing moments before held up their coats hoping to protect themselves. The police fired over seven hundred bullets while demonstrators fled for their lives. They did not stop shooting until there was no one left alive in the compound. The police said they were in serious danger because of stones thrown by the crowd. However, only three policemen reported being hit by stones.

When it was over, sixty-nine people lay dead or dying. At least another one hundred and eighty were wounded, including forty women and eight children. Most of the dead and wounded had been shot in the back. A South African newspaper, *The Rand Daily Mail*, reported:

The police opened fire ... volley after volley of .303 bullets and Sten gun bursts ... the hordes began to waver as scores of people fell before the hail of bullets. Soon they were routed. ... The police came out from behind the wire in front of the police station. Bodies lay scattered about. The wounded fled into backyards and side streets. Bodies lay in grotesque positions on the pavement. Then came the ambulances – eleven of them. Two truckloads of bodies were taken to the mortuary.

The Sharpeville massacre was international news within twenty-four hours. Grim photographs appeared in newspapers around the world – photographs that showed a field of corpses and two policemen with rifles standing guard. The world had its first image of South Africa under apartheid.

Afrikaner leaders publicly commended the police behaviour at Sharpeville, but international publicity had rocked the government. They tried to play down the event – but it didn't work.

Blacks staged strikes, held mass funerals that resulted in riots and joined protests and spontaneous demonstrations.

South African whites reacted immediately. The available supply of handguns and ammunition was bought up within days. Some towns formed commando units to

"THE SHARPEVILLE MASSACRE WAS INTERNATIONAL NEWS WITHIN TWENTY-FOUR HOURS."

protect themselves. There were frantic inquiries about leaving the country. The stock exchange experienced large-scale selling as international condemnation continued. By a vote of nine to one, the UN Security Council blamed the South African government for the shootings.

The government response to the demonstrations was swift. Helicopters hovered over white areas while army vehicles patrolled the grounds. Armed guards were posted at power stations to prevent sabotage.

A state of emergency was declared. The government, under Prime Minister Hendrik Verwoerd, now had the power to arrest or detain anyone who was suspected of subversion. Mere suspicion was enough – charges or proof were not necessary. Twenty thousand were detained. All public meetings were declared illegal as police arrested eighteen hundred political activists in nationwide raids. The ANC and the PAC were outlawed. Officially, the ANC no longer existed in South Africa.

Robert Sobukwe served three years in jail for incitement to riot. He was kept in prison for six more years without any additional charges being brought. He was then confined to his home until he died of cancer in 1978.

The Sharpeville massacre was a tragic climax in South African history. Black leaders now realized that nonviolent tactics were not enough. By 1961, the ANC had changed tactics. It had gone underground.

11
UMKHONTO WE SIZWE – SPEAR OF THE NATION

In 1961, South Africa became a republic and withdrew from the British Commonwealth.

In March of that year, Nelson Mandela made a surprise appearance at a convention of fifteen hundred black political activists. Defying government restrictions, Mandela delivered the main speech, his first public words since he had been banned nine years earlier.

By June, the ANC leaders were reassessing their policies. Violence, they concluded, was inevitable. It was foolhardy for them to practise nonviolence when all of their demands were met with brutality and force.

Meeting secretly with journalists, Mandela declared that "In my mind we are closing the chapter on this question of a nonviolent policy".

The ANC created a separate, armed wing: Umkhonto we Sizwe – Spear of the Nation. Spear was formed to combat, by using violent methods, the ruthless repression by the government. The failure of all nonviolent forms of protest left no alternative. Nelson Mandela was made commander in chief. He believed, as the Spear of the Nation manifesto stated:

> *The time comes in the life of any nation when there remain only two choices – submit or fight. That time has now come for South Africa. We shall not submit, and we have no choice but to hit back by all means in our power, in defence of our people, our future and our freedom.*

Mandela and the ANC leadership considered four forms of violence: sabotage, guerilla warfare, terrorism and open revolution. Sabotage was chosen because it would avoid taking lives. In addition, it would allow Spear of the Nation to affect South Africa's foreign capital and foreign trade. Spear's targets would be power plants, railways and telephone lines – all critical to the country's economy. By placing a severe strain on the economy, Spear hoped to convince voters to withdraw their support of apartheid. The organization enforced strict rules against injuring or killing anyone.

In December 1961, Spear struck government buildings in three South African cities. The explosions served notice that, indeed, the ANC had changed its tactics. Over the next three years, Spear recruited members and sent them out of the country to be trained to work with explosives.

Many ANC leaders, including Oliver Tambo, had already left the country. The ANC established headquarters-in-

A photograph taken of Nelson Mandela in 1962.

exile in Zambia. Mandela was smuggled out of South Africa to study revolutionary tactics and raise money in other African countries.

Mandela, by now a legend, was working underground. His ability to elude the police embarrassed the government. It seemed impossible that the easily recognized Mandela could go undetected. He took elaborate precautions, changing disguises frequently and using various aliases. One day he was a window washer, the next an errand boy. For a while he ventured out only at night. He walked busy city streets dressed as a night watchman or tribal healer, complete with beads and a painted face. He even appeared as a priest leading a funeral procession. Sometimes he only narrowly escaped. Once he had to slide down a rope from the second floor of a building. Another time he was spotted by a black policeman who walked toward him, gave him the thumbs-up ANC salute and walked away.

But the most difficult part of Mandela's decision to go underground was abandoning his family. When he left, he said only that he'd "be going away for a long time". When Winnie saw that he had paid the rent for six months and had the car fixed, she understood. Fortunately, after complicated arrangements, he was able to see her and sometimes the children. Those times would come, of necessity, without warning. A car would appear, and Winnie would be told to get in. After a while, another car would take over, and ten cars later she would be with her husband.

One time his disguise was so effective that she didn't recognize him at first. Sometimes Winnie and the children were able to meet Nelson at a farm in Rivonia, a town near Johannesburg. There Winnie would cook, and Mandela would take walks with his daughters.

But Nelson Mandela's luck ran out. He was betrayed by informers. The Verwoerd government paid well, and the bonuses they offered were hard to resist.

On August 5, 1962, after being a fugitive for eighteen months, Nelson Mandela was captured. The police had known precisely where to set up the roadblock that snared him.

He was sentenced to five years in prison with hard

labour. As the police van took Mandela away, the crowd chanted *"Tshotsholoza Mandela"* ("Struggle on, Mandela"). But Nelson Mandela's struggle was just beginning.

In the summer of 1963, the security police arrested Walter Sisulu and eight others on the farm in Rivonia. They also captured hundreds of documents and maps. Police informers who had infiltrated Umkhonto we Sizwe were again suspected of providing the government with information. The police had offered immunity from prosecution for any information. They had even placed ads for spies in black newspapers.

The captured evidence gave the government the proof they needed. In October 1963, the Rivonia Trial began. It lasted eleven tense and dramatic months. Nelson Mandela, already in jail, was again on trial – this time for his life. He was brought to the courtroom under heavy police escort. Guards armed with tear gas grenades were posted at every entrance. They kept careful watch inside also, where the galleries were filled. Winnie was there with Mandela's mother. The children, Zeni, now four, and Zindzi, three, were not allowed in the courtroom and had to wait outside.

Mandela was charged with recruiting and training for the purpose of sabotage and violent revolution. The registrar asked: "Accused number one, Nelson Mandela, do you plead guilty or not guilty?" Mandela responded: "The government should be in the dock, not me. I plead not guilty."

The government took five months to present their case.

Mandela had chosen to give no evidence in his own defence nor to allow himself to be cross-examined. He challenged the right of the court to try him in a country where he had no voice. He would, however, make a statement.

For Mandela, the trial was political, not criminal. On trial was white domination, not Nelson Mandela. His statement from the prisoner's dock is considered one of the most eloquent political speeches in modern history. He spoke for four hours.

He spoke of the suffering Africans endured because of apartheid:

South Africa is the richest country in Africa, and could be one of the richest countries in the world. But it is a land of extremes and remarkable contrasts. The whites enjoy what may be the highest standard of living in the world, whilst Africans live in poverty and misery ... in hopelessly overcrowded and, in some cases, drought-stricken Reserves, where soil erosion and the overworking of the soil make it impossible for them to live properly off the land. Thirty per cent are labourers ... and squatters on white farms, and work and live under conditions similar to those of serfs in the Middle Ages.

About the pass laws:

Pass laws, which to the Africans are among the most hated bits of legislation in South Africa, render any African liable to police surveillance at any time. I doubt whether there is a single African male in South Africa who has not at some stage had a brush with the police over his pass. Hundreds of thousands of Africans are thrown in jail each year under pass laws. Even worse than this is the fact that pass laws keep husband and wife apart and lead to the breakdown of family life.

About life in the townships:

Poverty and the breakdown of family life have secondary effects. Children wander about the streets of townships because they have no schools to go to or … no parents at home to see that they go to school, because both parents … have to work to keep the family alive. … Life in the townships is dangerous. There is not a day that goes by without somebody being stabbed or assaulted. … People are afraid to walk alone in the streets after dark. Housebreaking and robberies are increasing, despite the fact that the death sentence can now be imposed for such offences.

About the decision to turn to violence:

… without violence there would be no way open to the African people to succeed in their struggle against the principles of white supremacy. … We

were placed in a position in which we had either to accept a permanent state of inferiority, or to defy the government. We chose to defy the law. I did not plan it in a spirit of recklessness, nor because I have any love of violence. I planned it as a result of calm and sober assessment of the political situation that has arisen after many years of tyranny, exploitation and oppression of my people by whites.

About the argument against allowing blacks to vote:

It is not true that enfranchisement of all will result in racial domination. Political division, based on colour, is entirely artificial and, when it disappears, so will the domination of one group by the other.

About black education:

The complaint of Africans, however, is not only that they are poor and the whites rich, but that the laws which are made by the whites are designed to preserve this situation. There are two ways to break out of poverty. The first is by formal education. … The present government has always sought to hamper Africans in their search for education. One of their earlier acts after coming into power was to stop subsidies for African school feeding. Many African children who attend schools depend on this supplement to their diet. This was a cruel act.

"THE PRESENT GOVERNMENT HAS ALWAYS SOUGHT TO HAMPER AFRICANS IN THEIR SEARCH FOR EDUCATION."

About the way white South Africans look at black South Africans:

The lack of human dignity experienced by Africans is the direct result of the policy of white supremacy. White supremacy implies black inferiority. ... Menial tasks in South Africa are invariably performed by Africans. When anything has to be carried or cleaned the white man will look around for an African. ... Whites ... do not look upon

[Africans] as people with families of their own; they do not realize they have emotions ... that they want to be with their wives and children like white people ... that they want to earn enough money to support their families properly, to feed and clothe them and send them to school.

About what Africans want:

Africans want to be paid a living wage. Africans want to perform work which they are capable of doing, and not work which the government declares them capable of. Africans want to be allowed to live where they obtain work ... to be a part of the general population, and not confined to living in their own ghettos. ... Africans want a just share in the whole of South Africa; they want security and a stake in society.

About his personal commitment:

During my lifetime I have dedicated myself to this struggle of the African people. I have fought against white domination, and I have fought against black domination. I have cherished the ideal of a democratic and free society in which all persons live together in harmony and with equal opportunities. It is an ideal which I hope to live for and to achieve.

The front page of Cape Town's The Cape Argus *on June 11, 1964.*

But if needs be, it is an ideal for which I am prepared to die.

The judge took three minutes to deliver his findings. Mandela was sentenced to life imprisonment.

12
PRISONER #466/64

His prison identity card read:

> Nelson Mandela
> Crime: Sabotage
> Sentence: Life, plus five years

He was sent to Robben Island, the South African Alcatraz off the coast of Cape Town. Robben Island was the state's maximum security prison. No ships were allowed within a mile and escape was considered an impossibility.

Mandela was taken to the new isolation section, which was separated from other blocks by a thirty-foot wall. There were no white prisoners.

Mandela and thirty other political prisoners were the first to occupy the cells. Their names were written in the wet cement. Mandela's cell measured seven by seven feet and was lit by a single forty-watt bulb. There was a mat for sleeping and two blankets. He was awakened at sunrise, when he washed and shaved with cold water, and emptied his sanitary pail. With other prisoners he helped dish out their breakfast of tasteless porridge.

He was put to work in the limestone quarry. With picks and shovels they dug out the limestone slabs and lifted them onto the waiting trucks. In the summer, the lime reflected the rays of the sun, baking them in the giant quarry hole. In the winter, they were whipped by the frigid winds that blew off the ocean. The prisoners' hands quickly became blistered, and their eyes were soon gritty and stinging from the lime dust. At night their backs ached as they returned to their cells. Covered by the white limestone dust, they looked like ghosts.

They were also forced to work repairing roads and collecting seaweed that had washed ashore. They were not allowed to see newspapers or receive any news from the outside world. Letters were limited to five hundred words and could only be about personal and family matters.

Mandela was allowed to see his wife and family twice a month for thirty minutes. He and Winnie spoke to each other through tubes and saw each other through a Plexiglas window. To visit her husband Winnie first had to get permission from the minister of justice. She had to report to the police when she left her home and when she returned. She travelled a thousand miles to the prison, including a forty-five-minute ferryboat ride at the end. When she arrived, Mandela would hear his name called, and he would be marched to the visitors' section. Winnie

Mandela visiting his cell on Robben Island, 1994.

was required to sign an agreement that she understood the regulations. The police stood close by to make sure they did not talk about politics, conditions in the prison or people on the outside. If they did, the visit was terminated immediately. Even if it wasn't, an abrupt "Time's up" signalled the end of the half hour.

News of the outside world was obtained from inmates just arriving. Mandela risked punishment as he talked to them while hammering in the quarry. Any information was listened to eagerly and analysed endlessly afterward.

Prison did not change Nelson Mandela.

He continued his habit of exercising every morning. In the evenings he studied. He was studying law through the mail as well as educating himself about Afrikaner history and language. At one point, permission to study was withdrawn for four years. This was a particularly difficult decision for him to accept.

He would not give in to the monotony of prison life. Each day was treated as a new opportunity. Friendships were made and renewed. Experiences were shared and old stories told yet again. Most important, plans for the future were discussed.

In 1975, Nelson Mandela began writing his autobiography. He hoped that his story might help illuminate the goals of the ANC and inspire his fellow South Africans – especially the younger anti-apartheid activists involved in the struggle.

Writing at night and sleeping whenever possible during the day, Mandela wrote on paper smuggled into his cell. After four months of intensive writing, he had completed five hundred handwritten pages. They were divided up, wrapped in plastic, hidden in cocoa containers and buried in three different places in the prison's courtyard.

A year later, in 1976, the manuscript was smuggled off Robben Island and officially published in 1994.

Mandela helped many learn how to survive behind bars. He encouraged them to educate themselves. Other prisoners felt he had a natural air of authority. They listened to what he had to say. He continued to talk about what he had always talked about: unity among blacks and a harmonious, multiracial society. His younger fellow political prisoners were taken with his humility and tolerance.

Nelson Mandela was teaching a new generation of anti-apartheid activists.

He helped solve problems brought to him by South African tribal chiefs. He represented the prisoners, bringing their grievances to the authorities. He taught them to use whatever tools they had. They called hunger strikes, work slowdowns and other protests. His ability to conduct himself in a forceful yet dignified manner gradually won him the respect of the prison officials.

There was pressure to release Mandela from both outside and inside South Africa. The United Nations called for the release of all political prisoners in South Africa. *The New York Times* called them 'heroes and freedom fighters' – the 'George Washingtons and Ben Franklins of South Africa'. Helen Suzman, a white liberal member of the government, was tireless in her fight against apartheid. The Black Sash, a white South African women's organization, spoke out, as did *The Rand Daily Mail*.

There were improvements. A table was placed in the cells, and in the winter prisoners were allowed to wear a blanket while reading. There was hot water for washing and even a volleyball court, table tennis, chess and a movie once a month. Eventually, they won the right to do useful work, speak to one another and have better and more food. Newspapers were allowed, and the number of visits and letters was increased.

Despite his efforts Mandela became ill. Unable to lift the heavy limestone rocks, he was punished with six days in solitary confinement. The solitary cells were wet and cold, and he was given only rice and water to eat. He worked in the quarries for ten years before doctors recommended lighter work. During this time, his eyesight deteriorated because of the work in the quarries, and he developed a bad back. He was put on a salt-free diet because of his high blood pressure. He lost fifty pounds and turned a sickly yellow colour. It was rumoured that he was suffering from cancer.

But Mandela would not give up. He kept up his morale and continued to be self-disciplined, determined and confident. His courage could not, however, change the reality of his situation.

To Winnie he wrote: *Sometimes I feel like one who is on the sidelines, who has missed life itself.*

13

STEVE BIKO AND BLACK CONSCIOUSNESS

By the mid-1960s, it seemed the South African government had destroyed nearly all black organized resistance. Black leaders were in jail, in exile or banned. After the Rivonia Trial, the ANC had all but disappeared. Merely wearing the ANC colours could get you arrested. Whites no longer feared black protest. The government, with the opposition weakened, continued creating a society ruled by apartheid.

Thousands of blacks flooded the cities looking for work. Squatter camps were the result, and by the mid-1970s there were one and a half million people living in these camps. They were illegal cities of shacks built from cardboard, plywood and sheets of corrugated tin. There was no running water or electricity. Children suffered from malnutrition and people begged for food. Periodically the government bulldozed these camps. Residents in the squatter camps were also trucked to the isolated and overcrowded homelands.

Periodically 'black spots' were cleared out. 'Black spots' were black settlements that had spread within white-only areas. Those who had jobs in surrounding white areas could stay. The rest would be loaded onto trucks and dropped at the nearest homeland. Three and a half million black South Africans were moved this way. To many blacks, these massive uprootings came to represent the worst of modern apartheid. They became the cause of continual anger and bitterness.

The population of the homelands was doubling. Half of the black population (which meant over a third of the total population) was now living on thirteen per cent of South Africa's worst land – land that was now suffering from drought.

Black men in the homelands were desperate to feed themselves and their families. Unable to live off the land, they travelled incredible distances to find work. Many travelled two hundred miles or more each day to jobs that barely paid a living wage. Many left as early as four A.M., returning late at night only to begin again within hours. Fifty per cent were away from their homes for more than fifteen hours a day. Many more only got to see their families once or twice a year.

Ninety per cent of the white population lived in spacious suburbs. Most had never been to a township. They owned comfortable homes with swimming pools. Blacks cooked and served their meals, polished their cars, mowed their lawns and trimmed their hedges. While whites enjoyed a surplus of housing, the townships suffered a profound shortage. Sometimes as many as forty blacks lived in a

A village in Natal.

two-bedroom house. Health care, sanitation, education and social services were hopelessly inadequate.

In the mid-1970s, international criticism began affecting South Africa's business and financial affairs. Businessmen and financial leaders pressured Prime Minister Vorster to make changes. Under Vorster, some of the more visible examples of apartheid began to disappear. Segregation in public accommodations and transportation was no longer the law. Hotels, restaurants and cultural and recreational facilities were now permitted to serve all races. Blacks could attend any white university that would admit them. But the changes were cosmetic and not real. Vorster hoped to give the appearance of removing apartheid while not making any real changes. The most important laws – those concerning land, housing, jobs and education – remained.

There were other problems developing. Complicated problems that would affect all South Africans.

There was a growing labour shortage. Industry was becoming more mechanized, and the need for skilled labour was increasing. There were simply not enough white workers to do the job, and the situation promised to get worse. Professional, managerial and technical positions had to be filled if the country was to function properly. Even the government admitted that blacks had to be trained to fill these positions.

Afrikaners feared what they saw happening. They were concerned that blacks should continue to be kept in their place.

But not all whites felt that way. Some had always believed that major changes were needed, others that blacks should be treated equally only in some areas. Some changes, they admitted, were needed in the future.

But blacks, especially urban blacks, were tired of waiting for the future.

After years of relative inactivity, the simmering anger began to bubble to the surface. In 1973, there were signs of renewed resistance from factory workers. They demanded higher wages and called strikes even though they were illegal.

"BUT BLACKS, ESPECIALLY URBAN BLACKS, WERE TIRED OF WAITING FOR THE FUTURE."

New voices began to emerge. The most eloquent was that of Steve Biko.

Steve Biko was born in 1946 in King William's Town, Cape Province. His father was a government clerk. Biko's brother had been arrested in 1963. Biko, then seventeen, was interrogated and expelled from high school because of his brother. He began to resent white authority and question white participation in the black liberation movement. He attended a liberal Catholic boarding school and, in 1966, entered medical school. Soon he was elected to the Students' Representative Council and became involved in the National Union of South African Students. NUSAS was an anti-apartheid organization, but Biko was opposed to the fact that its leadership was mostly white. He and others broke away from NUSAS and founded the blacks-only South African Students' Organization (SASO). Biko, a brilliant speaker with a magnetic personality, was elected SASO's first president in 1969. He dropped out of medical school to lead the organization. His philosophy came to be known as Black Consciousness.

Biko believed oppression was a psychological problem. Black South Africans were suffering from an inferiority complex after years of domination by whites. Blacks needed to embrace their African identity if they were to become liberated. They needed to become self-reliant and look to themselves for leadership. This was the only way they would become strong. Biko felt that whites had no place in black organizations.

Biko established rural health clinics for blacks unable to travel to urban hospitals. He created community programmes that offered literacy classes and taught practical skills like making clothes. His goal was to help provide the means by which blacks could become self-reliant.

Black power was the cry in America's cities. The time of black power had come in South Africa, too.

As Biko became more politically active, his philosophy became more widely known. The government began to take notice. They were alarmed by the number of blacks who were being made politically aware by Biko's words. By 1973, he was banned. He was not allowed to leave his hometown, have anything he said printed and could not speak in public. No one could visit him, and he was not allowed to be with more than one person at a time. The security police harassed him for every offence, from traffic violations to breaking banning orders.

By the age of thirty, he was a legend in the black community. He was soon to become one of its martyrs.

On August 18, 1977, Steve Biko was jailed without trial for the fourth time. Twenty-five days later the police announced that he had died in jail.

International pressure forced the government to have an inquest. He had been interrogated for three weeks at security police headquarters in Port Elizabeth. Beaten senseless, he was left to lie shackled on the floor of his cell for three days. Although a civilian hospital was nearby, he was driven, while still in a coma, seven hundred and forty miles in the back of a Land Rover. He was given no medical attention and died the next day, September 12, 1977, at Pretoria Prison Hospital.

The inquest ruled that Steve Biko died of brain damage caused by a severe head injury suffered while in the custody of the security police. No one was held responsible for the murder.

"Biko's death leaves me cold", Minister of Police Kruger said.

Although police roadblocks prevented thousands from all over South Africa from reaching the funeral, twenty thousand angry, grieving blacks did attend. The funeral lasted six hours. Nearly a hundred whites attended and were unharmed despite the bitterness of the occasion. The

*Steve Biko's coffin being carried into Victoria Rugby Stadium
in King William's Town for a memorial service; almost 20,000
mourners thronged the stadium.*

United States, Britain, Germany, France and other countries sent diplomatic representatives.

Steve Biko had never advocated violence. His death by torture was viewed throughout the world as shocking and disgraceful.

Eight years later a special panel found two government doctors guilty of giving Steve Biko inadequate medical care. Their conduct was ruled improper. Neither served any time in prison.

14
SOWETO:
THE CHILDREN'S CRUSADE

Soweto. *South West Townships*: thirty-two square miles of slums spread out on a featureless landscape with mostly unpaved streets and poorly constructed single-story houses. Over half a million, mostly poor, black South Africans live there. It is the largest black urban community in all of southern Africa. There are some comparatively wealthy black South Africans who live in Soweto. They live in an area called 'Beverly Hills'. But most blacks live in typical township poverty. Tiny overcrowded houses are lined up on nameless streets littered with garbage. Each morning the residents of Soweto crowd into the trains and buses that take them to their jobs in and around Johannesburg.

On the surface, all was calm, under control. But beneath the surface, Soweto was a city of bitter, angry and frustrated people. They were like thousands of sticks of dynamite waiting for the spark that would ignite them. In early 1976, the spark was provided.

"THE REACTION TO THE GOVERNMENT ANNOUNCEMENT WAS IMMEDIATE AND ANGRY."

There were, of course, still the *old* complaints: the insulting pass laws, the inferior status caused by segregation, forced removals, poor wages, lack of jobs and housing.

But the issue that lit the the fuse was education.

Education was necessary if black South Africans were to have any hope of advancing. Without the proper education there would be no equality, no progress.

The South African education system spent very little money on black schoolchildren. Much less than what was spent on white children. White schools had computers, tennis courts and swimming pools. They had fewer students per teacher. Blacks were not even required to attend school. Almost twenty-five per cent of all blacks dropped out of school before year two – nearly eighty per cent before year eight. Black schools were not only segregated, they were inferior. They were not only inferior, they also taught blacks to accept inferiority as their proper place in life.

In January 1976, Prime Minister Vorster's government announced that some high school subjects would now have to be taught in Afrikaans (Afrikaans had become the official second language of South Africa fifty years earlier). The decision was made despite the fact that many teachers and their pupils could hardly speak the language. Black South Africans wanted to continue to be taught in English. English was the language of the United States and the Western world. English was the language of opportunity. Afrikaans was the language of their oppressor.

The reaction to the government announcement was immediate and angry. Black school board members resigned, while students refused to write their exams in Afrikaans. Many teachers were outraged, and students began striking in protest. A serious crisis was at hand.

On Wednesday morning, June 16, 1976, twenty thousand students gathered to demonstrate against this new government policy.

The march was spontaneous. No organization planned it and there were no leaders. Some students held signs: TO HELL WITH AFRIKAANS; STOP FEEDING US POISON EDUCATION; WE WANT EQUAL EDUCATION, NOT SLAVE EDUCATION. Some were as young as six or seven.

They were on a collision course with the police.

Like Sharpeville sixteen years before, there were no warning shots. No order for the crowd to disperse. "We fired into them. It's no use firing over their heads", one policeman said.

Hector Peterson, thirteen, was the first to die. He was hit from behind and then carried into a journalist's car and rushed to a clinic. But it was too late.

The police threw tear gas canisters into the crowd, but the angry people continued forward anyway. There were dead and wounded children and teenagers already on the ground – blood soaking their clothes. Some were picked up by fellow students. Other students, in a rage, were pelting police with bricks and bottles.

The demonstrators were frightened as bullets flew through the air and more students fell. But the crowd kept coming. They chanted slogans as they continued to move toward the police. Some were screaming hysterically, outraged at the violence surrounding them. Others courageously ignored the danger. They were enveloped by dust from the unpaved streets, and chaos was everywhere.

Young blacks from the townships had had enough of nonviolent responses to government brutality. Many were inspired by the idea of black pride and were more militant than their parents. It was time the government of South Africa heard a different black voice. One that was not committed to peaceful and patient progress. A voice fuelled by years of repressed anger. Unlike many of their parents, they were not afraid of the police. Violence was the only way. The freedom, the rights and the power they wanted

Thirteen-year-old Hector Peterson being carried by a fellow student after being shot by police; he was the first of 700–1000 people to die in Soweto.

would not be given to them by whites. They would have to fight for it.

The police were taken by surprise. They retreated, blocked the road with their vehicles and called in reinforcements. By midday, hundreds of heavily armed police had arrived. Helicopters hovered overhead, dropping tear gas as riot squads swung into action.

The students fled down the streets and into houses, some tripping and falling and being trampled by their frantic fellow students. Others fought back with rocks, schoolbags, and anything else they could get their hands on.

The fighting raged through the night. Parents, returning from work, joined their children. By dawn, fifteen hundred additional police prepared to enter the township. First reports were that the disturbances had been contained, but this was far from the truth. Reinforcements arrived until, by the third day, Soweto's streets swarmed with police.

Twenty-five people died the first day. Rioting and arson spread and turned Soweto into a battlefield. Police in camouflage uniforms with tear gas canisters, automatic rifles and shotguns barricaded streets. They patrolled the unlit streets in convoys, shooting in the direction of sounds coming from doorways and alleys.

Soweto was under seige. Troop carriers rumbled through the streets. The army had been placed on alert. Police vehicles were positioned in the hills overlooking the townships.

A dark cloud hung over Soweto. Fires were burning everywhere. The dead bodies were being dragged away.

Twenty thousand students in Soweto protested the government's policy requiring the use of Afrikaans in the schools.

Funerals turned into protests, with the police firing at the angry mourners. Small roving bands destroyed government installations, shops, banks and anything associated with white South Africa. A white man was dragged from his car and killed by the incensed students. The homes of black policemen were also targets of their fury. Streets were blocked by mountains of burning tires.

For three days the outcome was uncertain. Soweto was exploding.

The violence had begun to spread to other townships. Eight townships erupted, and that number doubled over the next three months. There were reports of disturbances from all over the country.

Within days, hundreds had been killed. Tens of thousands of students boycotted classes, and five hundred Soweto teachers resigned. The death toll was mounting as riots swept through black South Africa.

There were reports that a police sergeant had ordered his men to "fire at rioters because it would be easier to arrest them if they were wounded".

There were other reports. White civilians with high-powered rifles were said to be shooting into Soweto from the hills. When they returned to their white suburbs, they bragged about how many *kaffirs* they had killed. (*Kaffir* is an Arabic word meaning infidel, a person with no religious beliefs. Afrikaners contemptuously used the word to mean 'nigger'.)

A photograph of Hector Peterson's bloodied body being carried by his horrified schoolmate brought the story of the uprising into millions of homes around the world.

After fifteen months of unrest, the government was back in control. The cost in lives had been great. There were an estimated seven hundred to one thousand dead and twenty-four hundred had been arrested. The police didn't lose a man.

Soweto had changed South Africa.

The students had done something that had never been done before: confronted the government with every means available to them. The uprising was the most serious confrontation between blacks and the government in modern times.

Black South Africans no longer feared violence. Violence had now become part of their lives.

15

'SHE WHO STRIVES'

It had been more than ten years since her husband had been sent to prison for life. In that time, Winnie Mandela had begun to become a political leader in her own right.

For the past decade, she had been known as the wife of Nelson Mandela. But Mandela was behind bars, and the struggle outside continued.

Her first task was explaining the situation to her two growing daughters. The questions they asked were difficult to answer. They didn't remember their father.

It was impossible for her to be the kind of mother she would have liked to be. Her family, like her marriage, was destined to be different from most. Due to her increasing political activity, her children had to raise themselves. The South African government left them no choice.

Winnie Mandela had been gravely concerned about the plight of her fellow black South Africans even before she met Nelson Mandela. In 1958, she joined a demonstration against an earlier government ruling that forced women

Winnie Mandela with her two daughters, Zindzi and Zeni, outside the courthouse.

to carry passes. She was imprisoned for two weeks. Later she was prohibited from writing or publishing anything. She was accused of breaking a policeman's neck and charged with resisting arrest. Her reputation for being fearless was beginning.

One day in 1969, she was arrested at dawn in a nation-wide raid. Zeni and Zindzi, ten and nine years old, and their mother were asleep when police banged on the door and shone lights in the window. It was two A.M., and they were demanding to be let in. Winnie was able to take her two daughters to her sister's house before the police took her away.

She and the others were charged with supporting the banned ANC.

Witnesses at Winnie Mandela's trial had clearly been tortured and forced to give evidence against her. Even though the state withdrew the charges, she spent nearly seventeen months in solitary confinement. During that time, she was unable to write to her imprisoned husband.

Just weeks after her release, she was banned again, this time for five years: one of her sisters had visited her because she was ill, causing Winnie to be arrested for breaking her banning regulations.

In the years to come, Winnie Mandela was forced to endure being banned, placed under house arrest and detained without trial. Her children were persecuted and she was separated from them and from her friends. There was an endless list of restrictions. But things would get worse.

In another early morning raid, in 1977, heavily armed security police arrived at her house in Soweto. Others waited in her yard. They ordered her to pack. Then they drove her and sixteen-year-old Zindzi to Brandfort, a black location near a small Afrikaner farming community. The house, #802, had no electricity or plumbing. Winnie Mandela was banished to Brandfort for seven years. She was placed under house arrest every night, on weekends and holidays. She was allowed no visitors and could be with only one person at a time. Policemen lived on either side of her.

A Winnie Mandela supporter holds up a message of loyalty.

Her years in the remote farming town were depressing, tense, lonely and hard. She was cut off from all her friends. From anyone who knew her. The police harassed her without letup. Her house was firebombed.

In 1982, her banning orders were renewed for another five years.

In 1985, Winnie decided to disobey those orders. "The government has gone berserk", she said. "No more banning orders and exiles. They are eliminating people physically. And I have no reason to believe they wouldn't do the same to me". She and her family returned to their home in Soweto.

By 1985, Winnie Mandela had become an acknowledged black leader.

Like her husband, she was always ready to help others, to put aside her own hardships and lend a hand. And also like her husband, she radiated an inner calm despite the turmoil that surrounded her. And there was plenty of turmoil.

Winnie Mandela had become a controversial individual.

She was fiercely independent and outspoken. She became isolated from many of the black political groups. She represented to South African blacks the change to a more militant position. In a fiery speech at a funeral for blacks slain by the police, she vowed to take the violence that was flaring up in the black townships into the white suburbs. "With our box of matches we shall liberate this country", she said.

Winnie Mandela began her political career largely in Nelson Mandela's shadow. As South Africa entered the 1980s, she emerged as a leader with her own voice.

Much had changed since Nelson Mandela had been sent to Robben Island. In the black liberation movement, acceptance had given way to defiance; hope and patience had faded away and been replaced by pride and rage. It was a time of deep divisions and growing conflicts in black South Africa.

Winnie Mandela, too, had changed with the times. She, too, had become radicalized as she entered the 1980s – a time that would make all that went before it seem tame.

PART 4:
STATE OF EMERGENCY

16
"ADAPT OR DIE"

In 1980, South African prime minister P. W. Botha told white citizens they "must adapt or die". Apartheid as it existed, he said, could not continue indefinitely. Pressure to make changes was coming from a variety of sources.

Since the violence of the Soweto uprising, it was clear that blacks would no longer accept apartheid. That violence, and the international reaction to it, were causing profound problems for the government of South Africa.

There were increased demands from the international community of nations. Foreign investors and banks were insisting on political reform as the only way of stabilizing the economy. The country was suffering from an economic recession, the worst since the worldwide Great Depression fifty years earlier. The international anti-apartheid movement, which had increased in size and visibility, was another source of pressure.

Some changes did occur. Blacks could own homes and property in the townships whereas before they could

A pro-ANC demonstration in London.

only rent. Hotels, restaurants, parks, taxis, buses, lifts and theatres were desegregated. Electricity was put in some townships and some restrictions were eased.

But black as well as many international leaders were convinced the government was only trying to camouflage apartheid. The changes being made were visible but without substance. The real issues were left unchanged. Black leaders accused the government of allowing a handful of blacks to become successful to quiet international criticism. The government hoped to point to them as an example of how well the 'new' apartheid was working.

Another part of the plan was to simply make apartheid sound better. Homelands were no longer called that. They became 'self-governing states'. The pass laws were referred to as 'influx control' and then as 'controlled urbanization'.

The South African government tried to present apartheid as being in the best interests of all South Africans. But this new version of apartheid was recognized by most blacks as not much different from the old version.

The government reforms also angered white South Africans. The ruling National Party faced sharp criticism from its own Afrikaner voters.

The government was trying to walk a fine line. It had to convince whites that they would continue to dominate – that the country would not be turned over to black rule. Whites feared the changes they saw taking place. Of the twenty-eight million South Africans, there were only five million whites. The black population was growing five times faster than the white population. Whites were becoming even more of a minority.

At the same time, the government had to assure blacks, the international banking community and other foreign investors that genuine changes were being made.

The reforms fooled no one and satisfied no one.

In late 1983, a government announcement was again responsible for upheaval.

There was to be a new parliamentary structure. The country's other dark-skinned minorities would be allowed to participate in the government. South Africa's three and a half million 'coloureds' (people of mixed black and white ancestry) would have their own House in Parliament. South

Africa's one million Indians would also have their own House, according to the reformed constitution. However, the formula was such that the white House could always outvote the other two. It was the first time any nonwhite groups had been allowed even a token role in the government. The new parliament was approved by white voters in 1983. Elections for the new Houses were scheduled for 1984.

The new structure was another insult to the already seething black population.

Violence was once again building in the townships.

17

STATE OF EMERGENCY

In the summer of 1983, thirteen thousand people gathered to establish a new anti-apartheid organization. The election for the new parliament was the most recent issue that led to the founding of the United Democratic Front. The UDF was a multiracial organization. It endorsed the Freedom Charter, and Nelson Mandela was elected a patron. The UDF hoped to coordinate internal opposition to apartheid. Heated disagreements were threatening the unity of the black liberation movement. The UDF wanted to build a united democratic South Africa. Within months, hundreds of community groups had joined, and the UDF membership was estimated at one and a half million.

The government's policy of divide and conquer was working in spite of the efforts of the ANC and the UDF. Instead of black groups uniting against apartheid, they were becoming further divided as government repression continued. Many conservative blacks were at odds with radical blacks. Those who wanted to work with the government to find peaceful solutions were considered collaborators by most militant blacks. The Black Consciousness movement disagreed with the United Democratic Front. Inkatha, a Zulu organization, was involved in a bitter feud with the UDF. Middle-class blacks were resented by the majority of blacks, who were poor. The followers of Mandela were fighting with the followers of Biko.

A short time before, blacks needed only to concern themselves with their white enemies. Now they were at war with one another over tactics, strategies and philosophies.

After the 1984 elections for the new parliament, a wave of protests swept through the townships. Within two years, more than a thousand people were killed. Before the violence was over, the toll was estimated as high as five thousand.

A school boycott became semipermanent in many areas. The students were showing their support for the nationwide uprising. "Freedom first, education later" was the cry. For blacks, school was nearly nonexistent. Many would not see the inside of a classroom for three years. The army moved in and occupied schools and surrounded entire townships.

It was the beginning of the most prolonged rebellion the country had ever experienced.

Comrades, as some young township blacks were known, armed themselves with stones and homemade petrol bombs and used them in their confrontations with the police.

White South Africans were urging the government to

crush the rebellion as blacks took to the streets in awesome numbers.

On March 21, 1985, the twenty-fifth anniversary of the Sharpeville massacre, police opened fire on a crowd attending a funeral. Twenty-one were killed and hundreds wounded. The police claimed that their actions were necessary because bottled petrol bombs had been hurled at them. Reporters investigating the scene found no evidence of broken glass from the bottles. Worse still was the testimony of some that the police had killed the wounded lying on the ground and placed stones next to their bodies. Allegedly this was done to make people arriving on the scene think that they had been killed in the act of stoning the police.

In July 1985, Botha's South African government declared a state of emergency. The declaration was renewed every year for the next four years.

The state of emergency allowed the government to take extreme action.

Severe restrictions made it impossible for journalists to report the news. Previously, like South Africa's courts of law, the press had been allowed to perform its function relatively freely. Now, with the imposition of drastic censorship laws, the newspapers were unable to report the news.

Journalists, in order to file a story, had to be able to understand hundreds of vague laws. Laws that restricted what they might report. Laws that were purposefully vague so that reporters would always wonder if what they were writing could land them in jail.

"THE GOVERNMENT ALSO DIDN'T WANT OTHER COUNTRIES TO BECOME AWARE OF THE EXTREME MEASURES THEY WERE TAKING TO RESTORE ORDER."

Newspapers that were not pro-government began leaving blank spaces in the middle of stories. These spaces indicated to their readers that the material had been censored by the government. An article might have a headline that read SOMETHING HAPPENED IN A RESIDENCE ... followed by a blank space. Soon the minister of law decided that blank spaces, too, were subversive and would no longer be tolerated. An issue of *Time* magazine appeared on South African newsstands with four pages blank. Those were the pages that reported on the rebellion.

All news about the rebellion was censored. The government did not want white citizens to panic. White South Africans were the most heavily armed population in the world. They feared a black revolution and were ready for it. Five million whites legally owned thirteen million handguns. The government also didn't want other countries to become aware of the extreme measures they were taking to restore order.

In 1986, thirty thousand people were detained without trial, some spending as long as three years in jail. Many were children and teenagers. Most were tortured, and many died.

The power of the South African police had grown greatly in the past few years. No one knew precisely how many there were. The police used a number of techniques to torture black political prisoners. One, the 'airplane', had the prisoner hold his arms straight out at his sides and rotate them. He was beaten every time he put his arms down. In the 'refrigerator', the prisoner was thrown, naked and wet, into a cold room and left for hours, sometimes days. There were also electric shocks, fists, boots and truncheons. Some prisoners were as young as ten.

On June 6, 1988, nearly two million black workers stayed away from their jobs. The three-day nationwide protest was called by South Africa's two biggest non-white trade unions. In some places over eighty per cent of the black workforce did not report to work. Nationally, it was estimated that over half stayed home.

Seven people were killed the first day. Ten died in the violence before it was over. South African security forces stood guard at train and bus stations. This was done to prevent workers who wanted to go to work from being physically coerced to obey the strike.

It was the nation's biggest general strike. Commerce and industry suffered significant disruption.

On June 9, the government, as expected, extended the state of emergency for another year.

Violence continued to spread across the nation, with eruptions occurring in all four provinces. Unlike before, the violence was no longer confined to the townships. In hundreds of remote places across the country, blacks were striking back at the police and the army with anything they could.

Desmond Tutu, the first black bishop of Johannesburg, condemned the police actions: "Our people are being killed just like swatting flies. They don't even give out the names of the dead anymore". The government was arresting anyone it considered a threat to public order. There was a countrywide purge as the numbers of arrests grew daily.

And the violence continued.

In Alexandra township, twenty-three mourners died in clashes with police. The fighting lasted for four days. The township burned for four months.

Armed soldiers, freed of all restraints by the state of emergency, rampaged through schools, beating and shooting black students.

Millions of blacks were involved in the fighting. The police and the army occupied the townships to maintain

Bishop Desmond Tutu in 1984, when he was installed as the Anglican Bishop of Johannesburg; a multiracial group of about 2,000 attended the service.

order. Soldiers in combat gear patrolled in armoured vehicles, fingers poised on the triggers of automatic rifles.

Black South Africa seemed to be burning out of control.

Government-controlled television (the government, afraid that television would be a negative influence on South Africans, did not allow it until 1975) continued to cover the usual rugby matches. One white magazine published a political weather map showing the violence moving across the country as if it were a weather front. The Afrikaner papers that did cover the crisis reported only the destruction of government property or violence done by blacks to other blacks. They urged the government to use maximum force to restore law and order.

White journalists who dared to venture into the strife-torn areas did so at their own risk. Trips were planned like commando raids. They drove fast BMWs with sunroofs so that they could take photographs on the run. It was no longer safe to be white and be in a township. Being black wasn't a guarantee of safety, either.

Divisions within the black population had blossomed into bitter and deadly conflicts.

18

BROTHER AGAINST BROTHER

After the uprising in 1976, there was a government crackdown. Thousands of young black South Africans left the country. Many entered the ranks of the ANC-in-exile. There they were trained to become soldiers in the army of the Spear of the Nation.

By the mid-1980s, the Spear of the Nation had intensified its campaign of sabotage. Over a period of time, thousands of Spear soldiers secretly re-entered South Africa. In small bands they attacked power stations, railway lines, government offices and township police stations. They averaged six or seven strikes a month. Attacks on vital energy installations caused over seven hundred million dollars in damage.

The ANC once again was becoming a visible presence in South Africa. Their nonviolent philosophy of the 1950s and 1960s had been supplemented by a philosophy of making South Africa 'ungovernable'. The ANC instructed their followers to do this via their underground 'Radio Freedom'.

Amid the terror and hatred that was now daily life in the

townships, the people began to govern themselves. Out of the chaos, people's courts flourished. To some they were the places where young blacks dispensed justice irrationally. But some residents praised them. They took steps to stop random violence. They tried to stop petty criminality. A thief might be sentenced to clean up an empty lot filled with garbage and debris or to attend political education classes.

The comrades struck back at the police and army in a variety of ways. They made iron shields and protected themselves while stoning the police. They dug 'tank traps' three feet deep that stopped armoured vehicles from cruising the townships' roads. They used petrol bombs and the 'clothesline', stringing barbed wire across a road at the height of a soldier standing on top of an army vehicle.

But some who called themselves comrades were just out for themselves, taking advantage of the turmoil. Posing as comrades, they would go from house to house notifying people there was a bus boycott the next day. When the workers left to walk to work across the fields, they robbed them of their money.

Vigilante groups made up of black businessmen, government workers and policemen fought back. They tried to deny the comrades the right to govern the townships. One vigilante group called themselves the A-Team. (*The A-Team* was a top-rated show on national TV.)

Black collaborators were targets for revenge by comrades. Anyone suspected of working with the government was subjected to 'necklacing'. The victim of a necklacing had a car tyre that was soaked in petrol placed around his neck and set on fire. Comrades hoped this would make anyone who was thinking about working with the police think twice.

The townships were beginning to be divided into 'turfs', battled over in gang-versus-gang warfare.

19
THE WHOLE WORLD IS WATCHING

The permanent state of emergency shattered confidence in South Africa's economic stability.

International criticism increased, and the government was being scrutinized by countries all over the globe. Even those that had been friendly to South Africa condemned the state of emergency.

Twelve European countries withdrew their ambassadors. The Pope said that apartheid weighed on the conscience of mankind. In June 1986, a report was issued by the British government. It warned that serious steps needed to be taken, or South Africa could become the scene of the worst bloodbath since World War II.

A number of the country's largest business and industrial groups pressured the government to lift the state of emergency. They further urged the government to negotiate with black leaders and end apartheid.

There was an upsurge of anti-apartheid feeling in the

United States. Americans were shocked by the violence they were seeing on their televisions and reading about in their newspapers. Thousands of Americans, including eighteen members of Congress, had been arrested for picketing the South African embassy and consulates. Black civil rights leaders campaigned against apartheid, and some U.S. corporations were cutting back operations or leaving South Africa completely. Many Americans were pressuring their government to place economic sanctions on South Africa.

Economic sanctions are actions taken to penalize a country that is violating basic human rights. If sanctions work, they help force that country to change its practices. It was hoped that the financial effect of the sanctions would be too much for the economy to bear. In the case of South Africa, the government would then be forced to negotiate with leaders of its black population. Sanctions do not, however, always work. The target country can find many ways to get around them.

Nelson Mandela had called for sanctions twenty years earlier: "This increasing world pressure on South Africa has greatly weakened her international position and gives a tremendous impetus to the freedom struggle inside the country".

In the early 1980s, Botha's refusal to lift the state of emergency fuelled the international campaign for sanctions against South Africa. Because of the threat of sanctions and the violent disturbances across the country, foreign

In an effort to counter the surge of anti-apartheid feeling and the threat of sanctions from countries around the world, the South African government severely censored the international press.

governments and banks would not invest money in South Africa. American banks were being pressured by their depositors and shareholders. They wanted them to withdraw their investments in South Africa. Perhaps, the depositors and shareholders felt, this would force South Africa to make genuine and significant reforms in its apartheid policy.

In 1985, the Chase Manhattan Bank decided to call in its loan. British, German and Swiss banks also demanded immediate repayment of money they had loaned to South Africa. It was a significant step: the loans totalled thirteen billion dollars. The rand, the South African monetary unit, fell thirty-five per cent in value in thirteen days. It hit an all-time low.

Members of the United States Congress demanded that the government impose strict economic sanctions on South Africa. In October 1986, the Congress overruled President Reagan's veto and an anti-apartheid bill became law. Although it was not as tough as most black South African leaders would have liked, the bill did contain a number of restrictions. It prohibited new investments in South Africa; banned the import of steel, uranium and other valuable materials; and suspended landing rights in the United States for South African airlines.

The extreme measures taken during the state of emergency, and the government's failure to negotiate with black leaders, had caused apartheid to become a major international issue. The economic effects of this were grave. The country was facing a serious financial crisis – a crisis that questioned the wisdom of apartheid and had the potential to cause the economic collapse of the country.

Something had to be done.

PART 5:
FREE MANDELA

20
"I WILL RETURN"

One night in April 1982, Nelson Mandela was transferred from Robben Island. Winnie found out when she read about it in the newspapers. Later she received an official letter informing her that her husband had been moved to Pollsmoor Maximum Security Prison. His number was changed to D220/82. He was sixty-four years old.

Officially, no reason was given for the transfer. But many believed that Mandela's influence among arriving prisoners was the cause. Robben Island's reputation as Mandela University was disturbing to the government. He taught his young fellow prisoners to respect intelligence and learning. He organized a prison education programme and tirelessly and unselfishly shared his knowledge with his fellow inmates.

At Pollsmoor, Mandela continued his rigid routine of the last two decades. Each morning he exercised for two hours. He kept up with his studies and listened to the radio. The food was better than at Robben Island. But there wasn't the same sense of community at Pollsmoor.

Sergeant James Gregory had been assigned to guard Mandela at Robben Island. He was transferred along with his prisoner. Sergeant Gregory and Nelson Mandela had known each other for almost twenty years. A mutual respect had developed. Happily, visits from Winnie were more pleasant. They were allowed to touch for the first time since he had been imprisoned. When visiting time was almost up, the sergeant would kindly remind Winnie and Nelson Mandela.

Two years earlier, in a Pretoria bank, three men had taken twenty-five people prisoner. They demanded that Mandela be released in exchange for the hostages. The police stormed the bank, killing the three men and two of the hostages. The men were considered heroes by most blacks. Twenty thousand attended their funeral.

FREE MANDELA read the headline in a black South African newspaper earlier that year.

The leader of the Black Sash said: "We believe the most visible act of faith by the government would be to release Nelson Mandela".

The following week a photograph of Winnie and her daughter appeared under the headline: LET MY FATHER GO.

The campaign to free Nelson Mandela was under way.

The campaign began to attract worldwide support. The United States and Great Britain were pressing for the South African government to release the one man they felt

> ## "THE FOLLOWING WEEK A PHOTOGRAPH OF WINNIE AND HER DAUGHTER APPEARED UNDER THE HEADLINE: LET MY FATHER GO."

might solve the crisis. A United States congressional delegation requested to see Mandela, but the South African government refused. Honours and awards were pouring in from universities and human rights groups. Parks and streets were being named after him.

In 1984, a journalist was allowed to interview Mandela. Mandela had followed the violent eruptions of the past few years. He saw "no room for peaceful struggle" and "no alternative to violence". The conflict was destined to continue, Mandela said, unless the government took serious steps.

They must put an end to the homelands; allow blacks to have representation in the government; and implement a policy of one man, one vote.

Mandela also spoke about white fears of black domination. He did not want white South Africans to believe that black liberation meant that they would have to leave the country of their birth. Mandela was aware that many whites feared that the end of white domination meant they would have to abandon their homes. He took pains, as he had before, to reassure them. "Whites in South Africa belong here – this is their home. We want them to live here with us and share power with us".

In August 1988, Mandela was suffering from a bad cough and was having trouble speaking. He was hospitalized with tuberculosis. He might have caught it in his damp cell at Pollsmoor. Or, as some speculated, it might have begun as far back as his hard years on Robben Island. He was in pain and his appearance was shocking.

He was taken to one of the best medical centres in the country. By October, his condition had improved. There was a good chance he would recover completely.

Two months later, he was moved to a cottage at Victor Verster Prison. Victor Verster was a prison farm with a swimming pool. The government published photographs picturing the comfort Mandela was living in. They were the first photographs released since 1966 on Robben Island.

Mandela lived in a three-bedroom house over a mile away from the main prison building. On Robben Island

and in Pollsmoor, the companionship of his fellow prisoners had been important. Now, isolated, he was not allowed to leave his compound. He saw only guards. The loneliness was difficult to bear.

During Mandela's illness, high government officials were concerned that he might die while in prison. If that happened, they feared the increased violence that was sure to follow – violence they might not be able to contain as they had so far.

News of his illness brought renewed demands for his release.

By now, Nelson Mandela had spent more than half his adult life behind bars. He had become the symbol of the movement for black liberation in South Africa. Children who were not yet born when he was jailed cried his name. He stood for freedom to millions who had neither seen nor heard him. The overwhelming majority of black South Africans considered him their leader. Others, white as well as black, realized that only his release could end the crisis that was threatening to destroy their country.

Speculation about Mandela's release increased in the second half of the decade. The question became not *if* but *when*. When would the ruling National Party be willing for the first time to talk with black South Africans?

It was rumoured that Mandela was studying Afrikaans in preparation for the negotiations he hoped would finally come about.

But Nelson Mandela had been offered his freedom before and had refused it.

In January 1985, President Botha offered to release Mandela. Mandela, Botha stipulated, had to agree to a number of conditions. He had to formally reject violence and agree to live in the Transkei. The Transkei, the place where he was born, was now one of the so-called homelands. Officials of the government said they no longer stood in the way of a free Nelson Mandela; the choice was his.

On Sunday, February 19, 1985, Zindzi Mandela read her father's response to the government's offer. Ten thousand people had gathered at Jabulani amphitheatre in Soweto. The United Democratic Front was honouring Bishop Tutu, who had been awarded the Nobel Peace Prize the year before. Wearing the yellow T-shirt of the UDF, Zindzi, now twenty-five, told the audience:

> *My father and his comrades wish to make this state-ment to you, the people, first. ... My father says, "I am surprised at the conditions that the government wants to impose on me! It was only when all other forms of resistance were no longer open to us that we turned to armed struggle. ...*
>
> *"I cherish my own freedom dearly but I care even more for your freedom. Too many have died since I went to prison. Too many have suffered for the love of freedom. I owe it to their widows, to their orphans, to their mothers and to their fathers who have grieved and wept for them. Not only I have suf-fered during these long lonely wasted years. I am*

Zindzi Mandela read her father's response, a refusal of the government's offer to grant him a conditional release from prison.

not less life-loving than you are. But I cannot sell my birthright nor am I prepared to sell the birthright of the people to be free. ... What freedom am I being offered while the organization of the people remains banned? What freedom am I being offered when I may be arrested on a pass offence? What freedom am I being offered to live my life as a family with my dear wife who remains in banishment in Brandfort? What freedom am I being offered when I must ask for permission to live in an urban area? What freedom am I being offered when I need a stamp in my pass to seek work? What freedom am I being offered when my very South African citizenship is not respected?

"Only free men can negotiate. Prisoners cannot enter into contracts. … I cannot and will not give any undertaking at a time when I and you, the people, are not free. Your freedom and mine cannot be separated. I will return".

South African government officials continued talks with Nelson Mandela over the next four years. In early 1989, Mandela wrote to Botha: "The deepening political crisis in our country has been a matter of grave concern to me for quite some time, and I now consider it necessary … for the African National Congress [ANC] and the government to meet urgently to negotiate an effective political settlement". The stalemate, however, continued until late 1989.

In October, F. W. de Klerk was elected state president of South Africa. He had run for office on a platform that promised negotiations and a peaceful resolution to the country's crisis. Many in South Africa and in the international community favoured this approach. De Klerk presented a plan for a new constitution. Although he said he did not believe in integration, he did believe in accepting the inevitability of a multiracial state.

That same month, Walter Sisulu and seven other prisoners from the Rivonia Trial were released unconditionally.

In December, Mandela and de Klerk met and talked in Cape Town, at the president's office.

Residents of Soweto joyfully celebrate the release of Nelson Mandela.

In early February 1990, de Klerk made several stunning announcements:

- The ANC and sixty other organizations would be allowed to operate legally.
- Restrictions on three hundred and seventy-four people would be lifted.
- There would be a temporary halt to executions.
- The national state of emergency would soon be lifted.
- The government was committed to implementing a new constitution with no domination.

And, finally, the long-awaited announcement that the government would be releasing Mandela within days:

I am now in a position to announce that Mr. Nelson Mandela will be released at Victor Verster Prison. ... We would all like Mr. Mandela's release to take place in a dignified and orderly manner.

The news conference announcing that Mandela would be released was seen live throughout the world.

At 4:15 P.M., Sunday, February 11, 1990, Nelson Mandela was released from prison for the first time in ten thousand days. He was seventy-one years old.

21
"AMANDLA!"

Millions around the world heard Mandela address the fifty thousand people gathered in front of the Cape Town City Hall.

"*AMANDLA!*" Mandela chanted the Zulu word for power.

"*NGAWETHU!*" ("It is ours!"), the crowd responded.

This had long been the chant of the black resistance movement in South Africa.

"We have waited too long for freedom. We can wait no longer". The struggle, he urged, must continue on all fronts. There was no room for relaxing the pressures on the apartheid government.

He concluded the twenty-minute speech with his own words, spoken at the Rivonia Trial – words, he said, that were as true today as they were a quarter century before.

I have fought against white domination, and I have fought against black domination. I have cherished the

"ON THE DAY AFTER HIS RELEASE, EIGHTY THOUSAND FLOCKED TO A FOOTBALL STADIUM IN SOWETO BECAUSE OF RUMOURS MANDELA WAS GOING TO APPEAR."

ideal of a democratic and free society in which all persons live together in harmony and with equal opportunities. It is an ideal which I hope to live for and to achieve. But if needs be, it is an ideal for which I am prepared to die.

In the days and weeks following his release, Nelson Mandela, who had been named deputy president of the African National Congress, patiently explained the ANC's position. The first thing that had to be done was for the government to create a political climate in which negotiations could take place. They had to lift the state of emergency, release all political prisoners, repeal oppressive laws, end political trials and withdraw the troops from the townships. There would be no talks until the government met these demands.

On the day after his release, eighty thousand flocked to a football stadium in Soweto because of rumours Mandela was going to appear. He and Winnie had returned to their house on Vilakazi Street in Soweto. It was now surrounded by a four-foot-high brick wall topped by barbed wire. There were fears of assassination attempts by radical Afrikaners. Many of them felt that de Klerk, by freeing Mandela, was turning the country over to the blacks. The South African police worked with young blacks to guard the Mandelas' home. Reporters, photographers and TV vans were everywhere. The small house was crowded with people welcoming him home.

The months that followed were filled with activity. In

early May, the ANC and the government established a committee to study and make recommendations on the question of political prisoners. The ANC considered anyone who was in jail for fighting against apartheid a political prisoner. The government refused to recognize those who were convicted of murder, terrorism or arson as political prisoners. The issue emerged as a complicated obstacle on the road to full negotiations.

There were announcements from both sides. Both promised to work together to end the violence in their country. But as the talking continued, so did the violence.

In mid-May, the government announced that public hospitals would admit all South Africans, regardless of race. A month later, the state of emergency that had been in effect for the past four years was lifted in three of South Africa's four provinces. (The state of emergency remained in effect in Natal, where violence continued to erupt between black South Africans.) The forty-seven-year-old Separate Amenities Act was revoked. It had been one of the most significant of the apartheid laws. The act had legalized separate buildings, services and conveniences. Now South Africa's parks, beaches, swimming pools, services and public buildings were desegregated.

Mandela called the ending of the state of emergency a victory for blacks and whites, but he was cautious about the progress being made: "Twenty-seven years ago I had no vote; twenty-five years thereafter, I still have no vote, and that is due to the colour of my skin". He continued to stress the importance of maintaining the economic sanctions that had been imposed on South Africa by foreign governments.

Mandela and the ANC leadership worked to broaden their base of support in South Africa. Negotiations with the government were sure to be, at best, lengthy and difficult. Walter Sisulu, now in charge of ANC activities within South Africa, was concerned that "the youngsters are not really interested in the process of negotiations. ..."

Many disagreed with the ANC approach. Having grown up in an atmosphere of violence and government brutality, they believed that violence, not discussion, was the only response. They believed, as one slogan put it, that 'Revolution is the only hope of the hopeless'. The ANC was committed to reestablishing the organization as a commanding and visible presence in the townships. They, too, had slogans: ANC LIVES, ANC LEADS. Their goal, they pledged, was a negotiated settlement that would be a victory.

Both Mandela and de Klerk were aware that the drama of reconciliation in South Africa would, in part, unfold before a global audience. President de Klerk postponed his trip to the United States, fearing he would be overshadowed by Nelson Mandela's eagerly awaited visit.

The first week in June (only a day after he was discharged from a Johannesburg hospital where he had minor surgery) Nelson Mandela began a six-week trip to fourteen countries. His twelve-day, eight-city tour of the United States was the high point of the trip.

Security precautions for the arrival of Nelson and Winnie Mandela in New York on Wednesday, June 20, were as elaborate as any that had gone before. Twelve thousand New York City policemen, at a cost of two million dollars, were deployed to ensure Mandela's safety. The city was placed on a three-day traffic alert. Four bomb trucks, sixteen teams of demolition experts, helicopters, boats, mounted police and over six thousand wooden barricades were used for Mandela's ticker tape parade.

The Mandelas waved at the crowd (estimated between one and two million) from inside the specially designed bulletproof glass bubble – almost instantly known as the Mandela Mobile. Uniformed sharpshooters were strategically placed on rooftops along the parade route that ended with speeches in front of City Hall. Fifty thousand attended a rally at Yankee Stadium the next night.

There were private dinners with politicians and businesspeople, and cocktail party fund-raisers where supporters paid $1,000 and $2,500 to attend. Celebrities wrote large cheques to help increase the ANC treasury.

New York's newspapers welcomed Mandela with bold headlines that praised him as a hero and a freedom fighter. The Empire State Building was lit up with the ANC colours.

Before leaving New York, Mandela addressed a special session of the United Nations. He turned his attention to the critical issue of sanctions:

Nothing that has happened in South Africa calls for a revision of the position that this organization has taken. The sanctions that have been imposed by the

United Nations and individual governments should remain in place.

The next week, Mandela met for three hours with President George H. W. Bush. Again Mandela underlined the importance of maintaining economic sanctions. His address before a joint session of Congress was interrupted frequently by applause.

Nelson Mandela and U.S. President George H. W. Bush, 1990.

After visiting New York; Washington, D.C.; Boston; Atlanta; Detroit and Los Angeles, he ended his visit to the United States in Oakland, California. Summing up the trip that was clearly a moving experience for him as well as for the millions of Americans who welcomed him, Mandela said:

Despite my seventy-one years, at the end of this visit I feel like a young man of thirty-five. I feel like an old battery that has been recharged. And if I feel so young it is the people of the United States of America that are responsible for this.

PART 6:
THE STRUGGLE CONTINUES

22
UBUNTU

On July 18, 1990, his seventy-second birthday, Nelson Mandela returned from his triumphant world tour to a country where the overwhelming majority of the black population was besieged by long-term, seemingly insoluble problems: widespread political violence and crime (ten times as many people were killed annually in South Africa than in the United States, itself a violent society); deep-rooted poverty; poor housing, plumbing, electricity, and water supply; high divorce rates and incidences of teenage pregnancy; inadequate educational facilities that were minimally staffed by unqualified teachers and adult illiteracy.

Although now an internationally respected leader, he had no real power or authority within South Africa. His first task was to rebuild the African National Congress, which was now legal after being banned for thirty years, into a viable political party. During his travels, Mandela had generated much-needed funds. Now, with the help of

Nelson Mandela acknowledges the cheers of the crowd.

his comrades, he methodically moulded the ANC into the dominant political force in South Africa.

But that alone was not enough. Always the pragmatist, Mandela knew that the road to multiracial harmony would have to be paved with determination, compromise and cooperation. He knew he needed the support of black and white South Africans. His vision of a new, democratic, multiracial South Africa was inspired and driven, in part, by his lifelong understanding of the African concept of *ubuntu*.

Archbishop Desmond Tutu speaks of *ubuntu* as "the very essence of being human. ... It is to say, 'My humanity is caught up, is inextricably bound up, in yours.' We belong in a bundle of life. We say, 'A person is a person through other persons.' ... 'I am human because I belong. I participate. I share'".

Mandela made it clear in speech after speech that the South Africa he was envisioning was one that included people of all races and religions. His steadfast commitment to keeping his 'eye on the prize' of *ubuntu* ensured that negotiations between him and de Klerk, however troubling, disappointing and halting, continued.

President de Klerk took his time, for time was on his side. The longer he delayed, the more likely Mandela's international stature, which had increased immeasurably since his acclaimed release from prison, would be diminished, therefore affecting his negotiating strength.

Preliminary talks began in May 1990, but progress was slowed by the political violence that was worse now than at any time during all the dark years of apartheid. Perhaps most disturbing was the so-called 'black-on-black' violence involving members of rival black organizations: Chief Buthelezi's Inkatha Freedom Party (made up predominantly of Zulus) and Mandela's own ANC.

Mandela fruitlessly appealed to those involved in the fighting to "Take your guns ... your knives, your pangas and throw them into the sea".

Despite his words, he was faulted for his inability to do anything to control the two warring groups. Many white South Africans said this was what could be expected if blacks were to rule. If the ANC was incapable of controlling its own people, they asked, how could they be capable of governing the entire country?

Mandela charged de Klerk with responsibility for the fighting and accused him of not doing anything to stop the killing.

In an open letter to de Klerk on April 5, 1991, Mandela wrote:

... the country has witnessed a scale of bloodletting hitherto unknown. Estimates provided by agencies who have been monitoring the situation place the number of those who have lost their lives in excess of five thousand.

... Death and the destruction of homes and property on such a scale would be considered a national disaster in any sane society. The scale of human tragedy alone provides sufficient motivation for us to address you with our grave concerns.

The president didn't bother to reply. When negotiations first began, Mandela appeared to truly trust de Klerk, calling him a "man of integrity". But as time went on, he came to regret those words.

A newspaper story revealed that, as Mandela suspected, there was a 'third force' operating secretly within the government. This 'third force' was funding and fuelling the fighting in the hope that black South Africans would eventually kill one another off. The information in the article reflected poorly on de Klerk's perceived integrity and enhanced Mandela's.

The brutal fighting combined with the troubled economic state of South Africa threatened the negotiation process, the possibility of a democratic election and the very stability of the country. Many feared that South Africa was on the verge of civil war.

For a time talks ceased, but members of the government and the ANC met secretly, keeping the process going. Both sides begrudgingly made concessions. The government repealed the remaining apartheid laws, withdrew the hated emergency decree and released many political prisoners. Mandela, elected in July 1991 as president of the ANC, agreed to suspend the armed struggle.

Since his release from prison, Nelson Mandela was becoming more than a representative of the ANC. He was, in fact, becoming a world statesman. During 1990 and 1991, he carried the tale of South Africa's freedom struggle and his message of hope to more than twenty countries around the world. As a result of these visits, many countries insti-

Nelson and Winnie Mandela salute the crowd at the first ANC conference in South Africa in thirty years.

tuted sanctions against the government of South Africa, which meant that they would not sell any goods to South Africa or buy anything from it. The more recognition and support Nelson Mandela earned from the world community, the more powerful he became in his negotiations with the South African government.

By the beginning of August 1992, an ANC-led alliance was leading a massive campaign demanding a halt to government-supported attacks. More than four million people participated in demonstrations all over South Africa.

The campaign included a two-day national strike staged on August 3 and 4. Ninety per cent of the black workers refused to go to work, making this the largest political strike in South Africa's history. Business and industry were virtually shut down. The following day, August 5, more than 100,000 people staged a peaceful march on the Union Buildings, seat of government in Pretoria. Nelson Mandela addressed the demonstration and said:

Our country is passing through the most important phase in its history. The passing of the old order of apartheid rule and the birth of a new era of peace, democracy and justice is marked with trials, tribulations, and immense sacrifices.

... It should be now clear to all that an interim government of national unity is an urgent and critical step to take our country forward. Such a government can only be based on the political realities which reflect the sentiments of all South African citizens. Unless our country decisively moves forward to the establishment of an interim government, there will be no progress. ... Let unity, discipline and peaceful action become the hallmark of everything we do.

Viva peace! Viva democracy!

A month later, on September 7, government soldiers opened fire on an ANC rally in Ciskei Bantustan, killing thirty-one and wounding almost two hundred.

The pressure on the South African government and its president, F. W. de Klerk, to end its racial policies and the violence was increasing daily now. In addition to Nelson

Mandela's efforts and continued demonstrations by the ANC alliance, world governments were constantly urging reform and the elimination of apartheid with increased sanctions.

Finally, on September 26, 1992, a Record of Understanding was signed between Nelson Mandela and F. W. de Klerk. Meaningful negotiations on many of the South African policies that had oppressed the blacks for decades could now be reopened. De Klerk's government was forced to continue investigations into the allegations of torture of prisoners and abuse, beatings, shootings and killings of protesters.

It was obvious that the South African government was going to have to change its ways of dealing with black unrest. Open attacks on the democratic movement and the ANC were now witnessed by the world through television, and the economy was suffering.

In April 1992, Chris Hani, a popular black leader, was shot and killed outside his house by a white male assassin. An Afrikaner woman took down his registration number and dutifully reported it to the police, who apprehended the vehicle and the man within minutes.

Fearing yet another escalation of the already horrific violence, Mandela appeared on national television. In a calm and dignified manner, he spoke out against hate and prejudice, pointing out that it was a white woman who came forward in the name of justice. (The two men responsible were subsequently convicted.) The speech, poetic

Above: Mandela casts his vote for president. Below: Chief Justice Michael Corbett administers the oath of office of the president to Nelson Mandela, May 10, 1994.

and politically astute (especially when contrasted with de Klerk's silence on the matter), displayed Mandela's leadership qualities to white as well as black South Africans.

In early June 1993, it was agreed that national elections would be held in late April 1994.

At the end of 1993, Mandela and de Klerk were announced as joint winners of the Nobel Peace Prize.

In the early morning hours of Wednesday, April 27, 1994, South Africans began lining up at polling stations. Some had walked miles to get there and would patiently wait in line for hours.

Voting procedures were, at times, chaotic and corrupt. Some people voted more than once, and some were underage. Ballots didn't arrive when and where they were supposed to, and some ballot boxes were tampered with. But these irregularities were not enough to jeopardize the triumph of South Africa's first democratic election. Much-feared sabotage of the election by right-wing extremists did not materialize.

Nelson Mandela had proved to be a willing and wily campaigner. His ANC party won 62.6 per cent of the vote. Twenty million people turned out – 86 per cent of those eligible to vote. It was the first time Nelson Mandela had been allowed to vote.

On May 10, 1994, as the heads of forty-five states looked on and a billion people around the world watched on television, Nelson Mandela was inaugurated.

Out of the experience of an extraordinary human disaster that lasted too long, must be born a society of which all humanity will be proud. ... Never, never and never again shall it be that this beautiful land will again experience the oppression of one by the other.

So spoke South Africa's first black president.

23
TRUTH AND RECONCILIATION

President Mandela knew that an industrialized country like South Africa could not function properly without the professional, managerial and technical skills of the white population. He tried, therefore, to assure white South Africans that there was no need to pack up and leave the country.

He retained the white staff he had inherited and read an Afrikaner poem in his first speech to parliament. In the summer of 1995, he attended the World Cup championship rugby match in Johannesburg. South African rugby teams had been banned for years from international competition because of the government's racist policies, and it was the first time South Africa was hosting the event. Wearing the team's green-and-gold jersey, Mandela went out onto the field after the game and congratulated the victorious captain of the still nearly all-white team. The overwhelmingly white crowd responded by chanting "Nelson, Nelson". That night in Johannesburg, both white and black South

Supporters of Mandela and the ANC celebrate in the streets after Mandela won the presidential election.

Africans celebrated together, something literally unthinkable only a few short years before.

Mandela's very public attitude of racial inclusion went a long way toward convincing white South Africans that this was a government in which they could participate. But black South Africans began to wonder if he wasn't spending so much time reassuring whites that he had forgotten about his own people. Forgotten about poverty, crime and violence that plagued them still.

Mandela travelled the world, soliciting financial assistance and investment from other countries. He enjoyed his new international celebrity status, which allowed him to call on world leaders (as well as meet famous rock stars and Hollywood actors). He spent so much time visiting foreign countries that there were jokes made about him during the few times he *was* in the country.

He became a critic of U.S. foreign policy during the Gulf War and befriended some of America's enemies: Cuba's Fidel Castro, Libya's Muammar Qadaffi, Yasir Arafat and Saddam Hussein.

He travelled all over South Africa, pressing business leaders to donate schools, clinics, hospitals – anything to help relieve the poverty that was everywhere.

But his fame didn't change who he truly was. He still awoke early and, as he had in prison, made his own bed. He liked chatting with his staff and, when travelling, with his pilots and bodyguards and those attending the dignitaries he was visiting.

While in prison, Mandela had been concerned that he

might not recognize the world when he returned to it. To a degree he didn't. He was shocked by the pervasive superficial materialism that had become the dominant factor in American, European and now South African culture.

He enjoyed good health, especially for someone in his late seventies. Photographers, however, were not allowed to use flashes near him because of his eyesight, which had been damaged during his many years in prison.

His innate ability to charm people and his sincere interest in them won them over. His now internationally known smile just added to his appeal.

The job suited him – he had evolved into a public person. The man had become the politician – someone who knew that his destiny was to serve his country.

In 1995, he established the Truth and Reconciliation Commission (TRC), which was to become his most controversial decision. The TRC would grant amnesty to anyone who willingly stepped forward and admitted the full truth of their politically motivated crimes. They did not have to show remorse or ask forgiveness from the families of those they tortured and killed. HEALING OUR PAST banners were hung in the halls where the more than fifty TRC sessions were held. Mandela hoped that by hearing the truth, publicly aired and admitted fully, both white and black South Africans could finally put their brutal shared past behind them.

The family of Steve Biko opposed any thought of giving his killers amnesty. The severe beating and subsequent death of Mr. Biko in 1977 had unified and energized the anti-apartheid movement and resulted in worldwide attention being focused on South Africa. Biko's wife and son listened on headphones as the Afrikaans testimony of the five policemen was translated into English.

The police officers recounted his death in gruesome detail. They said that he sat in a chair without permission, was belligerent and attacked them. They were, therefore, defending themselves when he became violent and "accidentally rammed his head into the wall".

The TRC report said that the officers' testimony was "so improbable and contradictory that it has to be rejected as false". The officers, the report said, "had clearly conspired to conceal the truth of what led to the tragic death of Biko". The officers were denied amnesty because they did not admit to committing a crime, and it was thought unlikely that they would face any further prosecution.

The two years of testimony by the seven thousand people who had applied for amnesty – their seemingly never-ending tales of brutal and inhumane treatment of black South Africans by the police, the military, and by black organizations – shocked even veterans of the struggle like Nelson Mandela.

The testimony clearly pointed to the top, but de Klerk admitted nothing, issuing banal general statements and denying any guilt or even knowledge of the crimes. This, despite the fact that he had attended a cabinet meeting where plans to 'eliminate' opponents of the apartheid government were discussed. Eliminate, de Klerk responded, did not mean kill.

Many felt that the TRC did more harm than good. The unrelentingly horrific testimony reminded black South Africans (who needed little to remind them) of the brutality and pain they had endured and of the family members and loved ones they had lost; it showed how blacks – the ANC and Inkatha – had also killed wantonly; it allowed confessed murderers to now go free; it did nothing to compensate the victims for their losses; and it was viewed by most of the white South African population as accomplishing nothing but unnecessarily dredging up the past.

It is difficult, however, to conceive of a better solution to the problem of reconciling that dark past.

24
WINNIE

Of all the appearances before the Truth and Reconciliation Commission, none was more dramatic and compelling than that of Winnie Mandela.

Nelson Mandela had sacrificed much during his nearly three decades in prison. But his most painful sacrifice was the disintegration of his marriage and his distance from his children. Both believed they had lost him to 'the struggle'.

Winnie Mandela had been victimized by the apartheid government for years. She had been arrested time and time again and forced into solitary confinement for nearly a year and a half. During that time, she had become hardened and steely. While her imprisoned husband forged a philosophy of negotiation and reconciliation, she appeared to embrace violence as the only response to the racist regime.

Whether she was truly politically motivated or was merely striking out indiscriminately and without purpose was a question. Some even wondered about her sanity: had

President Mandela and his wife, Winnie, in Durban, South Africa, in 1991.

the years of mental and physical torture made her go mad? Others believed she was simply out of control.

For many black South Africans, however, she represented their anger and their outrage. Long considered the 'mother of the nation', Winnie Mandela had become, perhaps even more than her famous husband, a symbol of defiance.

While he was in prison, Mandela was deeply troubled by reports of his wife's radical and erratic behaviour. Many of his trusted comrades counselled him that she was a liability to the struggle. But Mandela knew full well that she, like him and so many others, had suffered unspeakable hardships at the hands of their white oppressors. He truly understood his wife's anger but could not accept her refusal to adhere to ANC party policy or the uncontrolled violence that had become associated with her.

Although conflicted, he stood by her in 1991 when she went on trial for the brutal 1988 killing of fourteen-year-old Moeketsi Stompie Seipei. The teenager had been beaten at Winnie's home and later had his throat slit by some of her followers. She was convicted and eventually given what many considered a too lenient two-year suspended sentence.

A year later, Mandela announced that he and Winnie were separating because their marriage did not really exist any longer. They were divorced in 1996.

But Winnie remained a vital and independent force in South African politics. She was appointed to a government post in 1994. She continued, however, to disobey ANC party leaders and became involved in suspicious, self-serving, lucrative business deals that damaged her reputation. Mandela was forced to dismiss her from her job in the government. Despite this, she became president of the ANC's women's league in 1997.

Appearing before the TRC to give testimony as to her role in the murder of Stompie Seipei, she appeared as arrogant, defiant and dangerous as ever.

Some of her supporters demonstrated outside, while others, wearing battle fatigues and red berets, lined up inside, intimidating witnesses who were going to testify against her. At least one witness demanded physical protection.

On the ninth day of testimony, Winnie took the stand

"A YEAR LATER, MANDELA ANNOUNCED THAT HE AND WINNIE WERE SEPARATING BECAUSE THEIR MARRIAGE DID NOT REALLY EXIST ANY LONGER."

and offered vague and unbelievable explanations for her activities and equally unbelievable denials of any knowledge of any wrongdoing. The TRC concluded that she had known of and had been involved in numerous criminal activities and was not telling the truth about her involvement in the death of Stompie Seipei.

Mandela, meanwhile, had fallen in love with Graça Machel, the widow of the former president of Mozambique. They were married in 1998 as Mandela prepared to end his five-year presidency.

25
BORN FREE

By 1999, the last year of Nelson Mandela's five-year term as president of South Africa, there were troubling signs.

The ANC leadership, now an integral part of the government, had perhaps too enthusiastically embraced the wisdom of big business, capitalism and the money that it generated. This resulted in bribery, corruption and abuses of power within Mandela's government.

Black businessmen, many of them veterans of the struggle, strove to become as wealthy as their white counterparts. They made millions on diamonds and platinum and competed to see who would become South Africa's first black billionaire. For them, business and watching their investments, while living in their gated, security-heavy communities, was the face of the future.

While a few blacks got rich, the overwhelming majority remained poverty-stricken: only one other country in the world – Brazil – had a greater gap between the rich and the poor.

The younger generation, in their twenties – the 'born free' generation – knew nothing of the struggle that Nelson Mandela had come to symbolize. They took the democratically elected multiracial government as part of their birthright, which now, indeed, it was. Like their counterparts in Japan, Germany, the United States, Saudi Arabia and Great Britain, they were more concerned with earning good grades, getting into the best schools and using their intellectual and professional skills to secure wealth and a comfortable future.

Mandela's administration made some improvements in education, adult literacy, sanitation, electricity and clean water. But housing problems and homelessness persisted while crime and violence, unchecked by the inept police force, continued to grow. Crime was no longer politically motivated; it was now driven by money: bank robberies, carjackings (twenty-five vehicles a day hijacked in Johannesburg alone) and drugs. There was a dramatic increase in white-collar crime and crime in white suburban neighbourhoods, where house burglaries were increasing.

White South Africans began to leave the country, taking their much-needed skills and capital with them. And crime was discouraging foreign investment, profoundly and negatively affecting the already unstable economy.

But perhaps one of the most tragic episodes in the country's history is the AIDS crisis, which continues today.

South African president Thabo Mbeki, right, in 2004.

Mandela's term as president ended in 1999. During that same year, the acquired immunodeficiency syndrome, known as AIDS, became the leading cause of death in Africa. The disease reached epidemic proportions in South Africa: twenty-five per cent of the black population was believed to be infected with the human immunodeficiency virus, or HIV, the virus that causes AIDS. When Thabo Mbeki was elected president in 1999, he inherited a country in the midst of a major health crisis. Sadly, he did little to help the situation.

Thabo Mbeki was the son of Govan Mbeki, one of Nelson Mandela's fellow prisoners on Robben Island. Thabo Mbeki was considered hardworking, intelligent, highly educated (he has a master's degree in economics) and sophisticated. He was also considered shy, solitary, formal, impatient and uncharismatic. Mbeki questioned accepted medical opinions about AIDS. He did not believe there was a link between HIV and AIDS. He refused to discuss AIDS publicly or educate the public about how it was spread. He virtually ignored its existence. Infection rates soared. Mbeki also questioned the effectiveness of HIV drugs and blocked them from being distributed. AIDS patients died quickly without the help of lifesaving medications.

"TWENTY-FIVE PER CENT OF THE BLACK POPULATION WAS BELIEVED TO BE INFECTED WITH HUMAN IMMUNODEFICIENCY VIRUS, OR HIV, THE VIRUS THAT CAUSES AIDS."

Mandela admitted that he could have done more to help the AIDS crisis during his five years in office and was highly critical of Mbeki's mysterious position. Mandela called for the use of condoms and urged Mbeki to educate black South Africans about the disease and the need to get tested for HIV. Mandela's position on AIDS education gained more urgency when his oldest son contracted AIDS and died. "Let us give publicity to HIV/AIDS and not hide it", Mandela said.

Mbeki and Mandela clashed about numerous issues, but the subject of AIDS drove them apart. Mbeki often refused Mandela's telephone calls, and Mandela refused to stand when Mbeki entered parliament in early 2002.

PART 7:
AFTER MANDELA

26
PRESIDENT JACOB ZUMA

Under Thabo Mbeki's rule, the ANC had forgotten what they once stood for and turned their backs on the people who had put them in power. By 2005, a struggle for power between Mbeki and the deputy president, Jacob Zuma, was tearing the ANC apart. In June, the struggle came to a head when Mbeki dismissed Zuma, charging him with fraud and corruption. Zuma denied the charges, and his supporters claimed he was being set up by Mbeki.

Later that year, Zuma was accused of rape and denied the charge. He claimed that the people accusing him of crimes were trying to ruin his political career. He was found not guilty a year later, but many people thought the controversy was enough to end his career. To others, however, Zuma remained very popular in the ANC party. In 2007, at an ANC conference, Zuma was chosen to be the party's president, beating out Mbeki for the role.

The next year, 2008, Mbeki resigned as president when a judge ruled that he interfered with Zuma's corruption case.

Jacob Zuma in Capetown, South Africa, 2008.

A temporary leader was assigned and Jacob Zuma was on track for the presidency in 2009. It was, by any measure, a remarkable political comeback.

However, the prospect of Jacob Zuma becoming president of South Africa worried many South Africans – especially businessmen, members of the black and white elite, journalists and political experts. They believed he was uneducated and uncivilized.

Zuma was a polygamist, a man with many wives. He had six wives and nineteen children. If elected, he would become the first polygamist to be president of the country. Some thought this would reflect poorly on South Africa. Zuma had taught himself to read and write. He was often politically incorrect and proud of it. He didn't drink or watch television – he claimed that TV was destroying the country. He was not well educated about AIDS. He was critical of same-sex couples. At political rallies, he danced traditional tribal dances and sang a revolutionary war song from his apartheid days, 'Bring Me My Machine Gun', which had become his personal anthem. Zuma's traditional practices were seen by some as outdated. They feared the modern South African world would not benefit from such a traditionalist president.

In July 2008, Mandela celebrated his ninetieth birthday. A rock concert was held on June 27 in London's Hyde Park, in Mandela's honour, and all proceeds went to Mandela's 46664 organization. 46664, named for Mandela's prisoner number plus the year he went to prison, promotes HIV/AIDS awareness and prevention. 46664 also works to fight other areas of social injustice.

There was also a private celebration for Mandela in Qunu, the tiny village where he was born. Mandela was joined by his wife, Graça Machel (it was, coincidentally, their tenth anniversary), and approximately five hundred family members, close friends and associates.

In a message broadcast over the radio, Mandela said: "We are honoured that you wish to celebrate the birthday of a retired old man, who no longer has power or influence".

Though Mandela's words may have been somewhat true – he no longer led in a position of power – he still had a lot of influence over South African citizens.

Someone as popular and powerful as Nelson Mandela

Crowds watch performances at Mandela's ninetieth birthday concert in London.

had to think long and hard before choosing whom to support in the presidential race. Although Mandela was known to disapprove of Mbeki's policies, he said nothing publicly in favour of Zuma during the conflict between Mbeki and Zuma.

It was unclear whom Mandela would back until April 19, 2009, when Mandela made a surprise appearance in Johannesburg at a 100,000-plus rally for Jacob Zuma.

Mandela and Zuma had been comrades in Umkhonto we Sizwe (or MK), meaning 'Spear of the Nation', the armed wing of the ANC, in 1961. Zuma eventually became head of the intelligence unit. In that role, Zuma was responsible for planning bombings and eliminating suspected spies and traitors. Later, Mandela and Zuma were both prisoners at Robben Island. Mandela's presence at the rally was a clear and moving sign that he was giving Zuma his blessing despite the controversy.

In May 2009, Jacob Zuma was elected the fourth post-apartheid president of South Africa, and Mandela attended his inauguration ceremony. At that time, and in the weeks to come, Zuma made it clear that he intended to return to Mandela's policies of white/black reconciliation and uphold the original principles of the ANC, mainly equal rights for all.

Zuma also spoke about South Africa's many problems, including the economic recession, lack of jobs, widespread poverty, high crime rate, high HIV and AIDS infection rates and widespread corruption within the government. He vowed he would take a hands-on approach and work closely with the opposition to focus on goals such as land redistribution, universal education, improved health services and crime prevention.

Many South Africans had come to believe that these problems were not adequately addressed during Mandela's five-year term. But tackling so many struggles would be hard for any leader and Mandela admitted, "It was more difficult to defend the freedom we have won, than struggling or fighting to gain it". Critics felt that, during his years in office, Mandela acted as a symbolic global leader. They felt he had used a hands-off approach to government during his presidency.

Mandela was faulted for his failure to confront the AIDS crisis in a timely and proactive fashion. In fact, it has been questioned whether all the money generated by the famous rock concerts found its way to the right people. During Mandela's term in office, the economic gap between the rich and the poor widened. It continued to widen under Mbeki and again under Zuma.

The Zuma administration has made some changes, notably in the finance and health ministries. There is now a growing black upper middle class in South Africa that is reaping financial rewards. However, fifteen million people are still classified as working poor. Nearly thirty per cent of the population is unemployed, with fifty-seven per cent living at the poverty level, many in heavily populated settlements without electricity, running water or adequate housing.

Despite the steps Zuma has taken to help his country, his administration still has a reputation for being corrupt. Critics argue that Zuma and the ANC party spend too much of the country's money in questionable ways to benefit themselves and not South Africa's citizens.

27
THE WORLD CUP

Nelson Mandela, a boxer and sports fan, believed that sports had the power to unite black and white South Africans.

Many sports are played in South Africa, but football is by far the most popular. It has always been the ideal game to play in the townships, because there is no need for equipment and it can be played barefoot. Any flat, empty land can work as a field, and even if there is no access to a football, a can or ball of rubber bands will do. Football felt like *the* South African sport, which is why Nelson Mandela felt very strongly about bringing the 19th FIFA World Cup to his country. He played a crucial role in making that a reality when he travelled to the FIFA headquarters in Zurich to convince the officials that South Africa would make a good home for the 2010 World Cup. He succeeded. FIFA selected South Africa over Egypt and Morocco to host the tournament.

Perhaps Mandela felt so strongly about hosting the

World Cup because of his experience at the 1995 Rugby World Cup games, which were played in South Africa. The tournament was held after his presidential inauguration, and he celebrated by attending a match in Johannesburg. This was a particularly noteworthy way to celebrate because Mandela had no passion for rugby and, in fact, did not know many of the rules. At the time, rugby was a sport with mainly all-white fans, and those fans felt that rugby was their 'religion'. Black South Africans, on the other hand, hated the sport and specifically hated the national team, the Springboks, who were seen as symbols of apartheid and segregated sports.

Mandela raising his hat in support of the Springboks at the 1995 Rugby World Cup.

When Nelson Mandela appeared at a rugby game in a green Springbok jersey, spectators of all colours looked on in awe. "Nelson! Nelson!" was chanted for minutes by the nearly all-white crowd at the stadium. It is estimated that another billion people watched on TV. Most people were very moved by Mandela's gesture – wearing the green jersey signalled Mandela's wish to unify black and white South Africans. The Springboks won! After the game, black and white citizens sang and danced in the streets, celebrating not only the win but also how far their country had come. This was a turning point in modern South African history and a legendary moment.

Because of this experience, Mandela understood firsthand the power that sports could have in unifying and modernizing a country. He wanted the opportunity to show a unified and modernized South Africa to the world. He also wanted the opportunity to show that a black-ruled African country was capable of an enormous organizational, technological and financial feat. He wanted to prove that his nation was ready to take its place on the world stage.

Similar to Mandela, President Zuma was a former football player and a vocal supporter of the game. While in prison, inmates wanted to participate in the game so much that they made the right to play football the main focus of their complaints to the warden. The prison agreed, and Zuma played football daily. Like Mandela, Zuma also felt a personal attachment to seeing his country host the world's largest football match.

As opening day, June 11, 2010, approached, everything

seemed to be on track. Six long years of planning, organizing, managing and building had paid off. The five new stadiums and the five refurbished ones were completed on schedule and were architecturally impressive. The transportation infrastructure – high-speed metro trains, bus routes, roads and airports – had been upgraded, improved and modernized. Each would be needed to move the expected 400,000 visitors from place to place. Because South Africa has one of the highest crime rates in the world, security would also be important. Forty thousand policemen were deployed, armoured personnel carriers patrolled the streets, courts functioned round the clock

Soccer City Stadium in Johannesburg, South Africa, site of the 2010 World Cup.

and a twenty-four-hour multilingual hotline was established.

Despite all of the successful preparations, some viewed the World Cup plans in a less favourable light. Yes, the project had been completed on time, but at what cost and to what end? Critics pointed to the wildly escalating costs. The World Cup planners had estimated millions but had, in fact, spent billions. This money would need to be paid by the taxpayers in a country where so many lived in severe poverty. Many questioned whether spending billions on stadiums was a good idea when millions of citizens were still in need of proper houses. An estimated 250,000 homes could have been built for each stadium – and ten stadiums were constructed.

Critics argued that Johannesburg had been temporarily beautified for the worldwide TV audience by forcibly evicting people from their shacks. Local vendors who could have benefited from the crowds could not afford the stiff FIFA registration fees.

Patrick Bond, director of the Centre for Civil Society, criticized the government's decision to host the World Cup. He stated that, in the end, only the elite in South African society benefited and not the majority of the population. A population that was, despite the World Cup and despite Mandela's and Zuma's visions, still forced to exist within one of the most unequal societies in the world.

Nelson Mandela was supposed to appear on the opening day of the tournament, but tragedy struck. Zenani Mandela, one of Mandela's nine great-grandchildren, was riding home with a family friend from a pre-tournament concert. Zenani's friend lost control of the vehicle and crashed into a barricade in the early hours of the morning, killing Zenani. The twenty-three-year-old driver was charged with a DUI and eventually acquitted.

Mandela may have missed the opening day, but he couldn't skip the entire World Cup. The tournament was too important to him. Despite the tragedy, Mandela and his wife, Graça, attended the closing ceremonies. Some reports indicated that he had been pressured by FIFA officials to do so. The 85,000 attendees gave him a thunderous ovation and serenaded him with plastic horns called vuvuzelas. Mandela was right to believe in the power of the World Cup. It became the most watched television event in history.

To a degree, the World Cup was an important opportunity for South Africa. The global media coverage helped redefine the country for many people. The perceived success gave many citizens a sense of national pride. It could be argued that the event paved the road to a new, positive future for the country.

"MANDELA WAS RIGHT TO BELIEVE IN THE POWER OF THE WORLD CUP. IT BECAME THE MOST WATCHED TELEVISION EVENT IN HISTORY."

28
HE BELONGS TO THE AGES

On July 18, 2012, Nelson Mandela celebrated his ninety-fourth birthday with his wife, children and grandchildren in the village of Qunu where he spent his childhood.

Mandela's birthday was a worldwide celebration. To honour his sixty-seven years of service to his country, people around the world performed sixty-seven minutes of public service. Habitat for Humanity, an organization that builds homes for the homeless, built sixty-seven new homes. Fourteen million students simultaneously sang "Happy Birthday" to Mandela.

U.S. President Barack Obama marked the occasion by saying:

Nelson Mandela's personal story is one of remarkable will, unwavering integrity and abiding humility. ... By any measure, Nelson Mandela has changed the arc of history, transforming his country, continent, and the world.

Volunteers repair a wall of the school that Mandela attended as a boy on Nelson Mandela International Day, 2012.

Since his appearance at the World Cup two years earlier, Mandela had not made many public appearances. His health had been a factor. He survived prostate cancer, but was later hospitalized with abdominal pains and a recurring lung infection.

In the early hours of June 8, 2013, Mandela's lung infection worsened. Despite the fact that his bedroom was equipped with medical facilities, an ambulance was called to take him to Pretoria's Mediclinic Heart Hospital an hour away. It arrived at his home at one thirty A.M., but broke down due to engine trouble en route to the hospital, forcing Mandela to wait for another ambulance.

Medical reports in the days and weeks that followed from the government, Mandela's spokesman, family members and anonymous sources were, at best, confusing. As a result, there was much speculation and numerous rumours about his condition.

President Zuma visited Mandela in the hospital and reported that he was in good shape. Zuma's assessments were questioned by some who saw films from April that showed Mandela to be unresponsive and ill. Reports began to surface that Zuma was in charge of all information coming from the hospital and that he wanted that information tightly managed, perhaps to avoid rumours and possible panic by the population.

Winnie Madikizela-Mandela accused Zuma and other ANC leaders of taking advantage of the situation and using her former husband for publicity. She and her eldest daughter said in a TV interview that reports that Mandela was on life support were untrue. By early July, other reports seemed to confirm that Mandela's condition was critical but stable.

Winnie and her two daughters complained of all the media coverage. Winnie described the media as being like "vultures waiting when a lion has devoured a buffalo, waiting there for the last carcass. That's the image we have as a family". She later added, "We don't mind the interest. I just think it's gone overboard".

Still, Mandela's life and his illness were of global importance. As a result, reporters pressured doctors for information, and photographers paid top dollar to rent apartments with balconies that overlooked the hospital entrance where huge crowds formed. No one wanted to miss a detail as this critical story unfolded.

South Africans consider Mandela much more than a leader or political figure. They were as outraged as the family by the insensitivity of the media. They expressed these feelings by yelling "Foreigner, go home" during what have come to be known as 'drive-by shoutings'.

Perhaps most disturbing were the serious disagreements that erupted among Mandela's large extended family, and were hotly debated in court and in public. One particularly bitter feud concerned the question of where Mandela ultimately would be buried. A judge ruled against Mandela's eldest grandson, who wanted the bodies of the three deceased Mandela children to be exhumed and reburied in Mandela's birthplace, Qunu. The very next day, local law enforcement officials broke a metal padlock with large pincers and retrieved the three coffins. This was a victory for the sixteen family members who brought the suit, and a defeat for Mandela's grandson. Mandela's wife is thought to have sided against the grandson. Both sides, however, accused each other of being motivated purely by money, as it is assumed that his burial site will, in the future, reap great financial rewards for his heirs.

Other financial disagreements include questions regarding Mandela's image. It is unclear who will gain financially

"SOUTH AFRICANS CONSIDER MANDELA MUCH MORE THAN A LEADER OR POLITICAL FIGURE."

from artwork created by Mandela and who owns his image. A similar dispute has arisen over Mandela's name. His great-grandchildren have created a wine label called House of Mandela and a clothing line called LWTF, which is a reference to his autobiography titled *Long Walk to Freedom*. Two of his grandchildren star in a reality show titled *Being Mandela*. These disputes raise important questions. Who deserves to make money on Mandela's name? What will his name mean in the future?

Nelson Mandela's hospitalization coincided with President Barack Obama's previously scheduled week-long trip to Africa. The two met briefly in 2005 when Obama was a senator. Obama has said that Mandela was an inspiration to him as a young law student and so he was honoured to write the introduction to Mandela's 2010 book, *Conversations with Myself*. Obama wrote, "His sacrifice was so great that it called upon people everywhere to do what they could on behalf of human progress. In the most modest of ways, I was one of those people who tried to answer the call".

On Sunday, June 30, 2013, President Obama visited Robben Island, where Mandela spent eighteen of the twenty-seven years he was imprisoned by the apartheid South African government. Escorted by eighty-four-year-old Ahmed Kathrada, one of Mandela's closest comrades and fellow prisoners, Obama stood inside Mandela's tiny, seven-by-seven-foot cell and toured the limestone quarry where Mandela, Kathrada and the others had been forced to work.

President Obama met with some of Mr. Mandela's children and grandchildren and spoke by phone with his wife, who spent most of her time at her husband's bedside.

At a dinner with South African president Jacob Zuma, Obama recited from 'Invictus', a poem that Mandela first read when he was on Robben Island, and reread and quoted throughout his life:

> It matters not how strait the gate,
>   How charged with punishments the scroll,
> I am the master of my fate,
>   I am the captain of my soul.

During this time, Mandela was said to be in 'critical but stable' condition. This term is sometimes used to describe a patient on life support. Because of this, there was widespread speculation in the media that the Mandela family

President Obama looks out the window of the Robben Island cell where Mandela was imprisoned.

was facing a dilemma shared by thousands of other families: when to take a loved one off life support.

The speculation regarding Mandela's health continued when two of Mandela's longtime comrades and fellow Robben Island prisoners, Ahmed Kathrada and Denis Goldberg, visited Mandela in the hospital. They reported that he could not speak because of a tube down his throat to aid his breathing. But, they said, he was able to communicate with his eyes.

Though perhaps not strong enough to celebrate himself, people celebrated Mandela's ninety-fifth birthday all around the world on July 18, 2013. There were tributes at the United Nations, which had, in 2009, declared July 18 Nelson Mandela International Day. In Times Square in New York City, excerpts from Mandela's speeches appeared on a giant screen. The Dalai Lama, former U.S. senator and secretary of state Hillary Clinton, actor Morgan Freeman (who played Mandela in the film *Invictus*), the astronauts on the International Space Station and many others sent greetings in celebration of Mandela's birthday.

Again, many people devoted sixty-seven minutes to acts of kindness and public service. In Johannesburg and other locations across the world, people joined hands and formed a human chain, a symbol of the interracial unity that Mandela stood for. People donated food, blankets, clothing and other items. Some people painted, cleaned, constructed and even installed computers in honour of Mandela's many accomplishments.

On September 1, 2013, Mandela was discharged from the hospital. He had always been a fighter in every sense of the word and this health battle seemed no different. Back in 1979, while a prisoner in Robben Island, he told his then-wife, Winnie, he had a strong will to live. It appeared that this still held true.

At his home on the outskirts of Johannesburg, Nelson Mandela continued to receive intensive medical care. He remained in critical and sometimes unstable condition due to a lung infection.

He was too frail to appear at the black-tie premiere of the film *Mandela: A Long Walk to Freedom* in early November. His wife, Graça Machel, and former wife Winnie Madikizela-Mandela did attend. At the champagne reception that followed, Ms. Madikizela-Mandela said: "We should remember where we come from and that this freedom was hard earned and that it was won at a very, very heavy price".

Mandela's daughter Zindzi spoke at a previous screening of the film: "When I watched the movie it was a very emotional moment for me. I found it quite therapeutic. It made me confront many emotions that I'd buried and refused to acknowledge. ... At the same time, the love that kept the family together comes through in the film."

A month later, on Thursday, December 5, 2013, South African president Jacob Zuma announced that ninety-five-year-old Nelson Mandela had died. He went on to say that there would be a memorial service on Tuesday, December 10, at the World Cup football stadium near Soweto, and that Mr. Mandela's body would lie in state until the following Friday.

On December 10, U.S. President Barack Obama and First Lady Michelle Obama, and a host of other world leaders, attended the memorial service. Other guests included British Prime Minister David Cameron, former president George W. Bush and his wife, former president Bill Clinton and former secretary of state Hillary Clinton, as well as former president Jimmy Carter.

Mandela was buried on Sunday, December 15, in the rural village of Qunu, his childhood home, as he had wished.

President Obama, clearly moved, paid tribute to the man he credits with inspiring his own commitment to political action. In the first statement Obama released after Mandela's death, he said:

We have lost one of the most influential, courageous and profoundly good human beings that any of us will share time with on this Earth. He no longer belongs to us – he belongs to the ages.

Through his fierce dignity and unbending will to sacrifice his own freedom for the freedom of others, Madiba transformed South Africa – and moved all of us. His journey from prisoner to president embodied the promise that human beings and countries can change for the better. ...

I am one of the countless millions who drew inspiration from Nelson Mandela's life. My very first political action, the first thing I ever did that involved an issue or a policy or politics, was a protest against apartheid. I studied his words and his writings. The day he was released from prison gave me a sense of what human beings can do when they're guided by their hopes and not by their fears. ...

We will not likely see the likes of Nelson Mandela again. So it falls to us as best we can to forward the example that he set: to make decisions guided not by hate, but by love; to never discount the difference that one person can make; to strive for a future that is worthy of his sacrifice.

" "MADIBA TRANSFORMED SOUTH AFRICA — AND MOVED ALL OF US. HIS JOURNEY FROM PRISONER TO PRESIDENT EMBODIED THE PROMISE THAT HUMAN BEINGS AND COUNTRIES CAN CHANGE FOR THE BETTER...." "

— PRESIDENT OBAMA, DECEMBER 5, 2013

Mandela receives applause from his colleagues at the United Nations in 1990.

CHRONOLOGY

1400–1600	European colonial powers establish trading posts along the coast of Africa
1600–1800	European nations begin exploring interior of Africa
1652	Dutch East India Trading Company establishes refreshment station on the southern tip of Africa (Cape Peninsula)
1779	Wars begin between whites and Africans
1806	Great Britain takes possession of Cape
1834–1838	Great Britain frees Cape slaves
1836–1854	The Great Trek. Boers establish the Transvaal and Orange Free State
1838	Battle of Blood River between Boers and Zulus
1867	Discovery of diamonds
1886	Discovery of gold
1899–1902	The Boer War
1910	Self-governing British-ruled Union of South Africa formed
1912	African National Congress (ANC) founded

1914	World War I begins
JULY 18, 1918	Nelson Mandela is born
1919	Jan Smuts, prime minister
1924	J. B. M. Hertzog, prime minister
1925	Afrikaans recognized as second official language
1931	Great Britain grants South Africa full independence
SEPTEMBER 26, 1936	Nomzamo Winifred Madikizela is born
1938	Mandela enters Fort Hare College
1939	World War II begins
1944	Mandela joins ANC, helps form Youth League; Mandela marries Evelyn Ntoko Mase
1948	D. F. Malan, prime minister; National Party comes to power; apartheid becomes official government policy
1950	Population Registration Act classifies all South Africans according to race
1951	Mandela elected president of the ANC Youth League; Group Areas Act assigns separate group areas
1952	Mandela appointed volunteer in chief, ANC Defiance Campaign; Mandela elected president, Transvaal ANC;

	Mandela and Tambo open first black law partnership in country
1953	Bantu Education Act – African education placed completely in government hands
1954	J. G. Strijdom, prime minister
1955	Congress of the People adopts Freedom Charter
1956	The Treason Trial – Mandela and 155 other defendants
1957	Nelson and Evelyn Mandela divorced
1958	Mandela marries Nomzamo Winifred Madikizela; H. F. Verwoerd, prime minister
1959	Robert Sobukwe founds Pan African Congress (PAC); Zenani (Zeni) Mandela is born; Bantu Self-government Act establishes homelands
MARCH 21, 1960	Sharpeville massacre
DECEMBER 23, 1960	Zindziswa (Zindzi) Mandela is born
1961	South Africa becomes independent republic; Umkhonto we Sizwe (Spear of the Nation), armed wing of ANC, founded
AUGUST 1962	Mandela captured, charged with incitement to riot and leaving the country illegally
NOVEMBER 1962	Mandela sentenced to five years in prison

JUNE 1963	Police arrest Walter Sisulu and eight others in Rivonia, seize documents outlining ANC plans
OCTOBER 1963	Rivonia Trial begins, Mandela charged with sabotage and attempting to overthrow the state
JUNE 1964	Mandela and eight others sentenced to life imprisonment
1966	B. J. Vorster, prime minister
1968	Steve Biko founds black-only South African Students' Organization (SASO)
1969	Winnie Mandela arrested with twenty-one others and detained five months
1970	Winnie Mandela's banning order renewed for five years
1976	Riots in Soweto and elsewhere
1977	Steve Biko dies in custody of Security Police; U.N. Security Council imposes arms embargo on South Africa; Winnie Mandela banished to Brandfort
1978	P. W. Botha, prime minister
1980	Coloured school boycott and riots in Cape Province; U.N. Security Council calls for Mandela's release
APRIL 1982	Mandela transferred from Robben Island to Pollsmoor Prison

1983	New parliamentary structure approved by white South Africans; United Democratic Front (UDF) founded
1985	President Botha offers to free Mandela; Chase Manhattan Bank calls in loan to South Africa; government declares state of emergency as riots continue
1986	United States passes anti-apartheid economic sanctions bill
1988	Nearly two million black workers strike; Mandela hospitalized for tuberculosis
JULY 1989	President Botha talks with Mandela
OCTOBER 1989	Sisulu and others freed unconditionally by new South African president, F. W. de Klerk
DECEMBER 1989	Mandela meets with de Klerk
FEBRUARY 1990	De Klerk legalizes ANC, announces that Mandela will be released
FEBRUARY 11, 1990	Nelson Mandela is released from prison
MARCH 1990	Mandela named ANC deputy president; police kill seventeen in Sebokeng
MAY 1990	Preliminary talks begin
JUNE 1990	State of emergency lifted in three of South Africa's four provinces; Separate Amenities Act revoked; Mandela begins six-week trip to fourteen countries

JULY 1990	Mandela returns to South Africa; Inkatha supporters kill thirty ANC supporters
JANUARY 1991	Mandela meets with Buthelezi – accord signed to end township violence; Convention for a Democratic South Africa (CODESA) meets to draft a new constitution; Mandela elected president of ANC
MAY 1991	ANC stops talks with government
JUNE 1991	Groups Areas and Land Acts repealed
JULY 1991	Mandela elected president of ANC; 'Inkathagate'
SEPTEMBER 1991	National Peace Accord signed
AUGUST 1992	Millions of workers participate in nation-wide strike
SEPTEMBER 1992	Government soldiers kill thirty-one ANC supporters in Ciskei Bantustan; Mandela and de Klerk sign Record of Understanding
DECEMBER 1992	De Klerk dismisses twenty-three army officers
APRIL 1993	Chris Hani assassinated
JUNE 1993	Date is announced for South Africa's first all-race election
DECEMBER 1993	Mandela and de Klerk jointly awarded the Nobel Peace Prize

APRIL 24, 1994	Nelson Mandela elected president in first nonracial democratic election in South African history
MAY 10, 1994	Mandela sworn in
OCTOBER 1994	Mandela addresses the United Nations
1995	Truth and Reconciliation Commission begins
1996	New constitution enacted; Nelson and Winnie Mandela divorced
1998	Truth and Reconciliation Commission report is issued; Mandela and Graça Machel marry
1999	Nelson Mandela retires from office; Thabo Mbeki becomes president
APRIL 2004	Thabo Mbeki re-elected
MAY 2004	FIFA announces South Africa to host 2010 World Cup
JANUARY 2005	Mandela announces son's death from AIDS-related disease.
JUNE 2005	Jacob Zuma dismissed as deputy president of South Africa
DECEMBER 2007	Zuma becomes president of ANC
JULY 18, 2008	Mandela celebrates ninetieth birthday
MAY 2009	Jacob Zuma elected president of South Africa; Mandela attends inauguration

JUNE 11, 2010	Mandela's great-granddaughter Zenani killed in car accident; FIFA World Cup begins in South Africa; Mandela presented with World Cup trophy and attends closing ceremonies
2010	Mandela's *Conversations with Myself* published; foreword by President Barack Obama
JUNE 21, 2011	U.S. First Lady Michelle Obama and two daughters visit Mandela
JUNE 27, 2011	*Nelson Mandela By Himself: The Authorised Book of Quotations* published
JANUARY 2012	ANC's 100th Anniversary celebration; Mandela does not attend
JUNE 8, 2013	Mandela rushed by ambulance to a Pretoria hospital
JULY 18, 2013	Mandela celebrates ninety-fifth birthday in hospital
SEPTEMBER 1, 2013	Mandela released from hospital
DECEMBER 5, 2013	Mandela dies

BIBLIOGRAPHY

BOOKS

Benson, Mary. *The Man and the Movement*. New York: Norton, 1986.

Crapanzano, Vincent. *Waiting: The Whites of South Africa*. New York: Random House, 1986.

Davis, Stephen M. *Apartheid's Rebels*. New Haven: Yale University Press, 1987.

de Villiers, Marq. *White Tribe Dreaming*. New York: Viking, 1987.

Duke, Lynne. *Mandela, Mobutu, and Me: A Newswoman's African Journey*. New York: Doubleday, 2003.

Farwell, Byron. *The Great Anglo-Boer War*. New York: Norton, 1976.

Finnegan, William. *Crossing the Line: A Year in the Land of Apartheid*. New York: Harper & Row, 1986.

Finnegan, William. *Dateline Soweto: Travels with Black South African Reporters*. New York: Harper & Row, 1988.

Francis, Stephen (author), and Rico Schacherl (illustrator). *Madam & Eve: Strike While the Iron Is Hot*. Johannesburg: Jacana Media, July 2010.

Francis, Stephen (author), and Rico Schacherl (illustrator). *Madam & Eve: The Pothole at the End of the Rainbow.* Johannesburg: Jacana Media, December 2001.

Francis, Stephen (author), and Rico Schacherl (illustrator). *Madam & Eve: Twenty: Celebrating 20 Years of South Africa's Favourite Cartoon Strip.* Johannesburg: Jacana Media, April 2003.

Gerhart, Gail M. *Black Power in South Africa.* Berkeley: University of California Press, 1979.

Giliomee, Hermann, and Lawrence Schlemmer. *From Apartheid to Nation Building.* Cape Town: Oxford University Press, 1989.

Goodman, David. *Fault Lines: Journey into the New South Africa.* Berkeley: University of California Press, 1999.

Gordimer, Nadine. *The Essential Gesture.* London: Penguin Books, 1988.

Harrison, David. *The White Tribe of Africa.* Berkeley: University of California Press, 1981.

Harrison, Nancy. *Winnie Mandela.* New York: Braziller, 1986.

Holland, Heidi. *The Struggle: A History of the African National Congress.* New York: Braziller, 1989.

Hoobler, Dorothy, and Thomas Hoobler. *Nelson and Winnie Mandela.* New York: Franklin Watts, 1987.

Hope, Christopher. *White Boy Running*. Garden City, NY: Doubleday, 1989.

Kahn, E. J. *The Separated People*. New York: Norton, 1968.

Lelyveld, Joseph. *Move Your Shadow*. New York: Penguin Books, 1985.

Malan, Rian. *The Lion Sleeps Tonight and Other Stories of Africa*. New York: Grove Press, 2012.

Malan, Rian. *My Traitor's Heart*. New York: Grove Press, 1990.

Maltz, Leora, ed. *People Who Made History*. San Diego: Greenha ven Press, 2004.

Mandela, Nelson. *Long Walk to Freedom: The Autobiography of Nelson Mandela*. New York: Little Brown, 1994.

Mandela, Nelson. *The Struggle Is My Life*. New York: Pathfinder, 1986.

Mandela, Winnie. *Part of My Soul Went with Him*. New York: Norton, 1984.

Manning, Richard. *"They Cannot Kill Us All": An Eyewitness Account of South Africa Today*. Boston: Houghton Mifflin, 1987.

Mathabane, Mark. *Kaffir Boy*. New York: New American Library, 1986.

Mathiane, Nomavenda. *South Africa: Diary of Troubled Times*. New York: Freedom House, 1989.

Meer, Fatima. *Higher Than Hope: The Authorized Biography of Nelson Mandela.* New York: Harper & Row, 1988.

Meli, Francis. *South Africa Belongs to Us: A History of the ANC.* Bloomington: Indiana University Press, 1988.

Mokgatle, Naboth. *The Autobiography of an Unknown South African.* Berkeley: University of California Press, 1971.

Morris, Donald. *The Washing of the Spears: The Rise and Fall of the Zulu Nation.* New York: Simon & Schuster, 1965.

Nelson Mandela Foundation with Umlando Wezithombe (illustrator). *Nelson Mandela: The Authorized Comic Book.* New York: Norton, 2009.

Oliver, Roland, and J. D. Fage. *A Short History of Africa.* London: Penguin Books, 1988.

Omond, Roger. *The Apartheid Handbook.* New York: Penguin Books, 1987.

Pakenham, Thomas. *The Boer War.* New York: Random House, 1979.

Roux, Edward. *Time Longer Than Rope: The Black Man's Struggle for Freedom in South Africa.* Madison: University of Wisconsin Press, 1964.

Russell, Diana. *Lives of Courage: Women for a New South Africa.* New York: Basic Books, 1989.

Sampson, Anthony. *Black and Gold.* New York: Pantheon, 1987.

Sampson, Anthony. *Mandela: The Authorized Biography.* New York: Knopf, 1999.

Sparks, Allister. *The Mind of South Africa.* New York: Knopf, 1990.

Stengel, Richard. *January Sun.* New York: Simon & Schuster, 1990.

Thompson, Leonard. *A History of South Africa (third edition).* New Haven: Yale University Press, 2000.

Tutu, Desmond. *No Future without Forgiveness.* New York: Doubleday, 1999.

Woods, Donald. *Asking for Trouble.* New York: Atheneum, 1987.

Woods, Donald. *South African Dispatches.* New York: Holt, 1986.

ARTICLES

'A Killer's Ignorance Adds Poignancy to Biko Case'. *New York Times*, January 12, 1999, p. A4.

'Officer Is Denied Amnesty in the Killing of Steve Biko'. *New York Times*, January 11, 1999, p. A8.

Daley, Suzanne. 'Panel Denies Amnesty for Four Officers in Steve Biko's Death'. *Time* magazine, November 28, 1994, pp. 52–62. *New York Times*, February 17, 1999, p. A4.

Gevisse, Mark. 'A Tycoon and His Conscience'. *New York Times Magazine*, June 9, 2002, p. 96.

Karon, Tony. 'Can We Still be Friends?'. *Time* magazine, July 7, 2003, p. 18.

Mewshaw, Michael. 'Cape Town'. *New York Times*, September 16, 2001, p. 66.

Shear, Michael. 'In Mandela, Obama Found a Beacon Who Inspired from Afar'. *New York Times*, June 27, 2013, p. A1.

Shear, Michael. 'Unable to Visit Mandela, Obama Honors Legacy'. *New York Times*, June 30, 2013, p. 1.

Upadhya, Ritu. 'Father of His Country'. *Time for Kids*, November 1, 2002, p. S6.

Walsh, Declan. 'As World Awaits News on Mandela, Tensions Rise over Media Swarm'. *New York Times*, June 27, 2013, p. A14.

DVDS

Invictus, directed by Clint Eastwood. Warner Video, 2009. DVD.

The Long Walk of Nelson Mandela, directed by Clifford Bestall. WGBH/Frontline in association with PBS, 2012. DVD.

Madiba: The Life and Times of Nelson Mandela, directed by Robin Benger. Canadian Broadcasting Corporation, 2004. DVD.

ABOUT THE AUTHOR

Barry Denenberg began his literary career working in various bookstores in New York City, Cambridge, and Boston. Subsequent management positions with national book retailers and publishing houses convinced him to become a writer.

He has written many critically acclaimed and award-winning books for young readers. His two most recent are *Lincoln Shot!* and *Titanic Sinks!*. His biography of Muhammad Ali will be published in 2014.

Barry is married to publisher Jean Feiwel; they have a daughter, Emma, and a rescued chocolate Newf named Holden.

PHOTO CREDITS

INDEX

Page references in *italics* indicate material in illustrations or photographs.

A

Africa, colonialism in, 19–21, 40; geography, *xii*, 1, *2*, 19

African National Congress (ANC), 14, 16, 36–38, 39–42, 43–47, 49–56, 65, 66, 67, 72, 73–74, 91, 109, *116*, 119, 144, 146, 149–151, 157–166; and the Congress of the People, 49, 50, 51, *51*, 52; and Defiance Campaign, 43–48; demands of, 162–163; in exile, 91; and Freedom Charter, 49, 50, 52–53; in government, 178, 185, 190; and IFP, 160; Mandela deputy president of, 149; Mandela president of, 161; *New Age*, 50; and nonviolence, 37, 42, 44–45, *45*, 65, 74, 127; outlawed, 72, 91, 157; as political party, 157–160, 190; and Spear of the Nation, 73, 127, 188; and Treason Trial, 52–56; and violence, 73–74; and whites, 38, 39, 40, 66–67; and creation of Youth League, 40, 42

Afrikaans language, 30, *37*, 101, *105*, 141, 172; 185

Afrikaners, 16, 30, 32, 35, 39, 49, 64, 70, 94, 117, 149, 164, 168

AIDS, 179–180, 181–182, 187, 189

Alexandria township, 124

Alice, 7

anti-apartheid laws, and U.S., 130–133

apartheid, 16, 28, 30–32, 36, *37*, 38, 43, 46, 57, 70, 78, 89, 91, 92, 94, 115, 116, *116*, 117, 119, 130, 147, 160, 174; reform, 93–94, 115–118, 146, 150, 161; world reaction to, 46, 71, 115, 117, 130–133, 152, 168

B

banning orders, 47; and Nelson Mandela, 47, 48, 51, 53, 61, 73; and Steve Biko, 96; and Winnie Mandela, 109, 110

Biko, Steve, 95–98, *98*; banned, 96; family of, 171–172;

K

Kathrada, Ahmed, 202, 203

L

land ownership, 28, 29, 94, 115
London, *116, 188*

M

Machel, Graça, 177, 187, 196, 204
Malan, D. F., 30, 43
Mandela Children's Fund, 182
Mandela, Evelyn Ntoko Mase, 14, 15
Mandela, Nelson, 5–9, *8*, 144–154; and AIDS, 180–181, 182, 187, 189; and ANC, 14, 16, 38, 39, 48, 50–56, 74, 149, 157, 161; arrests, 46, 48, 52, 76–77; autobiography, 88, 201–202; banned, 47, 48, 51, 53, 61, 73; and boxing, 14; Cape Town speech, 147–149; childhood, 5–9; children, 14, 63, 76, 77, 86, 107–109, *108*, 138, 142–144, 180, 205; and Congress of the People, 50–56; and Defiance Campaign, 43–48; and de Klerk, 144–146, 160; disputes surrounding, 199–201; divorces, 15, 176; and economic sanctions, 131, 150–151, 162, 164; education, 6, 7, 9, 12; extended family, 195–196, 200–201; followers, 120; and free-Mandela campaign, 138–139; and Freedom Charter, 50–56; honours and tributes, 187, 197, *198*, 203–204, 198–200, 202–203, 204; illnesses, 89–90, 140–141, 151; and IFP, 160; in Johannesburg, 10–12, 15; law practice, 15–16, *16*, 57, 63; marriage, first, 14, 15; marriage, second, 61, *62;* marriage, third, 177; and miners, 10–11; movies, 204–205; name, 5, 9; in New York City, 151–153; and Nobel Peace Prize, 166; and nonviolence, 44–46, 73; political activity begins, 7–9; presidential elections, *165*, 166, 167, *169*, 187; as president, 166–168, 170–171, *175*, 177, 178, 179, 180, 182, 189–190; in prison, 85–90, 107, 111, 137–138, 140–141, 202, *203*, 204; refuses freedom, 141–144; release from prison, *145*, 146; after release from prison, 147–150; as retired president, 182, 187–188, 189; return to Soweto, 149; and Rivonia Trial, 77–84; separation from Winnie, 176; and Spear of the Nation, 73–74; and Treason Trial, 53–54, *54*, 55–56, *56*, 57–58, 59, 61; underground, 75, *75*, 76; and UDF, 119; and U.N. address, 152, *186*; at university, 7, 9, 12; U.S. Congress address,

Q

R

S

voting rights, 30, 80, 140, 150, 166

W

wages, 82, 94, 100
white domination, 28, 36, 40, 78, 81, 96, 117, 140, 147
white-only designation, 28, *37*, 45, 92, 93
whites, 2, 5, 11, 28–29, 30, 40, 78, 92, 117, 140, 179, 183; and ANC, 36, 38, 39, 40, 67; in black organizations, 66, 95; and blacks, 21, 38, 40, 64, 65–66, 81–82, 93, 94, 140; and conquest of Africa, 19–25; education, 100–101; and jobs, 29; and Nelson Mandela, 66; and parliament, 118; and Youth League, 40
white supremacy, 32, 79, 81–82; and Boers, 22; and Great Trek, 22–23
women, 107–108, 176
World Cup, 168, 191–196, *192*, *194*, 198

X

Xhosa language, 5, 7, 51
Xhosa tribe, 20, 23

Y

Youth League, 40, 42, 43, 66

Z

Zulu tribe, 23–25
Zuma, Jacob, 185–187, *186*, 188–189, 190, 193, 199, 202, 205